FROM TRIBAL DIVISION TO WELCOMING INCLUSION

From Tribal Division to Welcoming Inclusion: Psychoanalytic Perspectives provides a fascinating contribution to our understanding of the increasingly polarized and divisive nature of global politics. By describing the significant role of early mental mechanisms in interactions between the individual and society, the book offers a unique understanding of how our early mental life explains the social, cultural and political positions we assume later.

Splitting and projection are early defences meant to shield the growing mind from unbearable aspects of reality, but they also hinder our capacity for open-minded thought, and in contributing to the dangerous atmosphere of "us versus them", introduce tribal myths of an innocent group and external persecutors. The book illustrates these distortions of reality using a range of vignettes, notably the myth of white supremacy and the savage legacy of the Civil War in the United States. Gaining support from the work of Wilfred Bion, the book emphasises the need for integration of mind and the restoration of our capacity to face painful realities, including one's own violence and hatred.

This psychoanalytic study provides a balm for turbulent times. It will be of great interest to researchers and interested readers in the broad field of psychoanalysis, as well as those in the fields of political science, cultural studies and anthropology.

Maxine K. Anderson, M.D., is a Training and Supervising Analyst for several psychoanalytic institutes in North America. She is also a Fellow of the International Psychoanalytical Association, and a Fellow of the British Institute of Psychoanalysis. She teaches and practices psychoanalysis in Seattle, Washington.

FROM TRIBAL DIVISION TO WELCOMING INCLUSION

Psychoanalytic Perspectives

Maxine K. Anderson

Routledge
Taylor & Francis Group

LONDON AND NEW YORK

First published 2019
by Routledge
2 Park Square, Milton Park, Abingdon, Oxon OX14 4RN

and by Routledge
52 Vanderbilt Avenue, New York, NY 10017

Routledge is an imprint of the Taylor & Francis Group, an informa business

British Library Cataloguing-in-Publication Data
A catalogue record for this book is available from the British Library

Library of Congress Cataloging-in-Publication Data
A catalog record has been requested for this book

ISBN: 978-0-367-11019-2 (hbk)
ISBN: 978-0-367-11037-6 (pbk)
ISBN: 978-0-429-02443-6 (ebk)

Typeset in Bembo by
Servis Filmsetting Ltd, Stockport, Cheshire

For all our endeavors to learn and to grow:
Valiant efforts shaping our humanity
Comprise a fragile vessel
Often to be swept away by the flooding emotion
That is both the fount of our creativity
And the torrent of our inhumanity.

MKA June, 2018

CONTENTS

Acknowledgements   ix
Foreword by David A. Carlson   xi
Preface   xiv

Introduction   1

PART I
The mind may distort reality in order to maintain
security and stability   **5**

1   The myth of white supremacy   7

2   Seeking security amid emotional turbulence   30

PART II
**The mind faces feared realities: rescue via courage
and attentive care**   **41**

3   Seeking security via CARE and thought   43

4   Lessons derived from CARE, courage and self-respect   52

5   Transformations via trust in the as-yet unknowable   62

6   Appreciating the pain of integration   68

7   Summary reflections   74

References   *78*
Index   *86*

ACKNOWLEDGEMENTS

Appreciating how the openness and generosity of family, friends and colleagues are crucial for the emergence of creative efforts, I would like to cite here some who deserve special recognition.

Among close friends and colleagues, Mary Kay O'Neil has brought her talent for clarity and brevity to enhance the manuscript considerably. David Carlson has lent his wide-ranging lens, expressed in the Foreword to offer enriching perspectives and connections. I feel honored for his contribution. Catherine Kimble's very attentive reading and creative suggestions have helped to highlight not only certain details, but some of the book's overarching themes as well. Ladson Hinton, III, has offered fruitful discussions including some differing perspectives from those embraced by the book. His openness and candor have led to important re-considerations which I have tried to address. Nancy Wolf's thoughtful offerings have triggered new insights. I feel deeply grateful to each of these dear colleagues whose efforts are an expression not only of the mutual respect we share but also of their concerns for the issues the book hopes to bring to the reader's awareness.

In addition, Jack Ringel's significant sharing of his group experience enlivens the description of group mentality significantly.

And deep thanks to Russell George and Elliott Morsia at Routledge whose responsiveness has been so helpful in the details around submission of the manuscript.

And my husband Al Francisco has my undying gratitude. His wide-ranging, nearly inexhaustible reading has always been an invaluable resource. His generosity of time, patience, and technical skills in overseeing preparation of many details of the manuscript have been very beneficial. And his presence at all phases of the project has been of inordinate value.

FOREWORD

In this extraordinary book Maxine Anderson enlists today's news to explore and to illustrate the timeless forces that divide us, not only within ourselves, but also as citizens, as members of ethnic or class groups, or even as psychoanalysts pursuing one or another theoretical perspective.

A wide-ranging but carefully chosen series of psychoanalytic, social psychological and neuroscientific findings that illuminate early psychological development make a strong case for her account of what underlies group/tribal hatreds. In a beautifully modulated way, she describes why some of us are more prey to such hatreds, the situations that drive us toward more primitive attitudes toward others, and developments and interventions that help us surmount such destructive, embittered feeling and thought. Her considerations may help protect and enhance the effectiveness of a thoughtful citizenry in current times.

Dr. Anderson derives her psychoanalytic thought especially through Bion and relies heavily on the concepts of splitting and projection. How the deleterious aspects of these can be overcome through attentive mothering or through attentive listening, as in a good psychoanalysis, leads then to her own concept of CARE.

CARE is based on Dr. Anderson's previous book, *The Wisdom of Lived Experience* (Anderson 2016), where she described the mother's understanding, tolerant presence and involvement through the whole range of her child's behaviors, as highlighted by her caring patience in the face of the toddler's rage attacks. Her example deftly captures the kind of function that is internalized by the successfully reared child, thus dramatizing the sustaining, ultimately organizing effect of a parent's enduring attentiveness.

Philosophers will be among those interested in CARE, whose legacy in each person is one of synthesis and hence underlies and makes possible Hegel's thesis-antithesis-synthesis. CARE also captures and exemplifies Kierkegaard's "bearing witness," and carries forward the care aspect of Heidegger's *Dasein*. Ultimately CARE is the basis in the individual for the Empedoclean view of Eros that Freud introduced in *Beyond the Pleasure Principle* (Freud 1920). It's not that this work is grounded in philosophy so much as it is that it offers a view of what makes philosophical reflection possible and worthwhile.

In more specifically psychoanalytic matters, CARE can be seen as a developmental experience that is a nidus for early and persistent psychological development compatible with our various schools of thought. She comes close to Loewald's (Loewald 1971) account of internalization; and CARE will resonate similarly with ego psychological, interpersonal, relational, and self-psychological points of view as well as with observational studies. And while CARE is based on internalization, it stops short of Loewald's account of instincts as such, being organized through interactions within a psychic field consisting originally of the mother-child psychic union.

The special value of CARE, then, lies in capturing developmental views that diverse psychoanalytic schools and child developmentalists share and, as in the case of Loewald's work, eschewing what would provoke disagreement, e.g., in this case, the view of instinct as a consequence of interaction. Thus, CARE is a prime candidate for "common ground" of psychoanalytic work. It contains within itself room for further work and further specification and at the same time serves as a base from which our various schools can chart their own paths without losing contact with a clear common base.

On top of all this, we have a book that deftly characterizes our current political and social-economic malaise, with suggestions for emerging from it.

This is that rarest of works, a book that through its clear and accessible concept of CARE can provide the base for further psychoanalytic thought even as it serves to clarify and offer some hope for our current political and social situation. It will be an important addition to the library of every psychoanalyst and every dynamic psychotherapist and should command a wide readership among the educated public.

References

Anderson, M. K. (2016). *The Wisdom of Lived Experience: Views from Psychoanalysis, Neuroscience, Philosophy and Metaphysics*. London: Karnac.

Freud, S. (1920). Beyond the Pleasure Principle. *The Standard Edition of the Complete Psychological Works of Sigmund Freud*, ed. J. Strachey. London: Hogarth Press and the Institute of Psychoanalysis, XVIII.

Loewald, H.W. (1971). On Motivation and Instinct Theory. *Psychoanalytic Study of the Child* 26: 91–128.

David A. Carlson, M.D.
Clinical Professor of Psychiatry
Yale University School of Medicine
Training and Supervising Analyst
Western New England Institute for Psychoanalysis

PREFACE

Early in 2016, I wondered whether we were on the cusp of a monumental change from tribal suspicion toward more global inclusion. Subsequent events (e.g. the election of Donald Trump) and the ensuing divisiveness, have left me wondering whether we are descending into deep-seated hatreds that significantly close down space for thought. Was this a descent from the possibility of discourse to barely contained emotions—a danger not only for the individual and nations, but potentially for the planet?

In this book I attempt to explore the nature of these hatreds, and their social and emotional underpinnings. As a psychoanalyst I will offer the view that understanding the universal human triggers of violence embedded in tribal hatreds may lead us toward compassionate recognition of, and thus recovery from, their grip. The resulting capacities for considered thought, I will suggest, do bode well on two counts. One, is that thought fosters space for continued evolutions toward appreciation of diversity as a source for nourishment. Secondly, considered thought fosters the preservation of truth as based on objective facts as opposed to the contemporary 'post-truth' suppositions which reflect emotion and intensely held belief.

Fear and hatred of otherness is a state of mind. For example, white supremacy in the United States exemplifies intransigent polarization—a myth of white superiority based on black slavery.[1] This assumption of white purity and goodness, relying on the disavowed hatred and brutality felt toward the black underclass and fueled by shame-based honor, leads to distortions of reality and the incapacity for reflective thought. Early mental mechanisms meant to shield the vulnerable personality from unbearable realities comprise the psychic underpinnings of this myth.

The mental mechanisms of splitting and projection function in multiple ways to offer creative and protective division and differentiation of the mind. But they may also short-circuit the mind's capacity to appreciate the dilemmas and uncertainties inherent in complex reality by reverting to the simpler view of right and wrong, black and white, good and evil. This attempt to simplify reality by way of polarized positions, actually cleaves the mind, introducing violence by way of intensely negative emotions such as terror, fear and hatred. Projection relocates these painful affects into others, in a desperate attempt to contain the splintered mental fragments, while also attempting to keep the violent disturbance at a distance. Exploration of the power of the splitting processes, then, may offer some understanding of how protective mental functions may spread and maintain pain, hatred and derision, while also leading to paralysis of creativity and clarity of thought.

As an antidote to the fear and hatred of otherness, the concept of CARE is introduced as a source of restoration of mental integration. The inborn anticipation of one's needs being cared for, crucial to my sense of what comprises CARE, has consequences for personality development when these needs are met, but also when they are not met. Additionally, the capacity for emotional receptivity, another quality of CARE, is necessary for the development of reflection, empathy and compassion. Development of such qualities can transform violent affects triggered by polarized views. Emergence from entrenched polarization involves the courage to face disavowed truths, and concomitant denied pain. Suffering the pain of confrontations with denied aspects of the self, without emotional collapse, is crucial for integrating the mind. Further this creative suffering deepens the capacities for reflective thought and appreciating uncertainty. This greater depth bypasses earlier protective barriers and appears to foster trust and faith in what cannot yet be known. This transformative process integrates those aspects of mind and experience that the mechanisms of splitting and projection put asunder. Examples of mourning the loss of simpler views and the transformation of facing painful truths and emotions are offered to support the views proposed in this book.

Note

1   Baldwin (1965).

INTRODUCTION

Reality is more complex than we can envision. When science brings new understandings, such as the realization that we live in an expanding universe, we may embrace that new evidence. But, if such knowledge exceeds our capacities, we will let it fall from awareness, to maintain ourselves as intelligent, perceptive individuals.

Similarly, when it comes to self-understanding we protect ourselves with imagined certainties about who we are and what we know. Most of us navigate the world via our imagined realities based on loyalties to groups, cultures, traditions and personal temperament. A closer view may reveal how orderly growth and development aids swimming upstream against the entropic forces that sweep all of nature toward disorder and decay. As well, awakenings, derived from ancient parts of the brainstem, which fuel all our emotional and cognitive growth,[1] may inundate us. As creatures evolving in the midst of turbulence, we seem to need the equivalent of an attentive mind to receive our distresses, and to buffer us from these tensions. Interestingly, nearly the entire cerebral cortex, that most recently evolved part of our brain, is dedicated to gentling, labelling, and differentiating meaning from these otherwise chaotic internal and external environments.[2]

A further complexity is to realize how much our emotions impact the reality we experience. We believe that we clearly perceive the world about us as well as our inner selves. It may be difficult to consider that our unrestrained emotions and impulses likely shape our perceived reality. These inner up-wellings may generate tensions that trigger protective polarizations within us as individuals, groups or nations. When this occurs the inner space for calm thought is replaced by pressure. Initial stages of the mind's development, then, are often in conflict with subsequent thought-based functioning.

The mental mechanisms which organize the growing mind by way of creating categories may also violently cleave it into more simplistic functioning. The more complex aspects of reality, then, such as the creative uncertainties about oneself, as well as the outer world, are more difficult to comprehend than the seeming simplicities offered by certainties concerning self and others. To this less evolved state, the reversion to tribal functioning, which offers absolute certainties (such as right and wrong, us and them) may seem to provide safe harbor from the now-seeming external dangers of the new and the unfamiliar. As human history suggests, this more primary mode of relating to reality has been bedrock for millennia.

Recently, however, there may have been a shift in this pattern. The first half of the 20th century continued the violent legacy of the bloody conflict and inhumanity of two World Wars. During the second half of the last century, however, in sober reflection upon efforts to forestall repetitions of the carnage of those wars, leaders in Western democracies began to engage in an increasingly liberal progressive agenda. That is, a shift toward inclusion of otherness, rather than reversion to tribal animosities. The European Union, (1992)[3] with porous national boundaries and freer travel among member nations, offers an illustration. Further examples include the Arab Spring (2010),[4] and initial northern European openness to massive immigration from Africa and the Middle East (2015).[5] In the United States, perhaps the boldest recent example of a shift toward diversity has been the two-term election of a black Democratic president, Barack Obama, (2008–2016), fostering liberal policies. Certainly, there has been alarm and backlash toward these events, e.g. the Brexit vote to leave the European Union (2016)[6] and the Trump election (2016).[7]

Some of these backlashes may be understood as reversions to the less complex reality of polarized positions. It is also important to consider the outrage of working-class voters who have felt overlooked by the liberal agenda, especially, perhaps, in the United States. The diminishment of national borders in the case of Europe, or efforts to attain racial equality in the United States, raise serious questions about the loss of distinctive identities. Close examination suggests that for some, identity seems to pivot on remaining distinct from other groups. Keeping boundaries distinct, and closely identifying with tribal loyalties is often based on race. Here, there is a fear of intrusion, imposition, or being over-run. Diversity is not felt to be enriching. Difference endangers one's traditional values rather than nourishes via new perspectives and ideas. The Brexit vote suggested this concern.[8] Also, Barack Obama's election to the White House, and his carrying forward the liberal agenda toward globalization and inclusion left many working-class Americans feeling bypassed and overlooked.[9] Obama's election, as well, challenged the white supremacist dictate of black subjugation. It seems to have triggered significant "white lash," fueled in part by the tacit encouragement for hate-based groups by his presidential successor.[10] For example, Donald Trump, apparently appealing to his base of support, made incendiary remarks and failed to denounce the neo-Nazi and white supremacist movements following the riots in Charlottesville, Virginia in August, 2017.[11]

This fear- and hate-based movement and its history may reveal some of the psychological underpinnings that perpetuate such negativity. Understanding some of these inner workings and their origin in human development may also aid us in looking clearly at the violence and inhumanity which such entrenchment has long denied. It appears that only by facing the difficult truths, long hidden in over-riding myths, can emergence from such entrenchment occur.

In addition, appreciation of how such emotional intensity inundates space for thought may illuminate the contemporary "post-truth" phenomena as based solely on powerful emotion.

Finally, recognition of this internal violence involves mourning the lost myth of perfection. But this process may also offer transformation of fear about survival into welcoming openness. The pain of mourning and ownership of this violence seems to sculpt inner psychic space sufficient to provide not only space for quiet thought, but trust in ourselves, each other, and our created institutions. Rather than reversion to automatic suspicions, such faith fosters an atmosphere of mutual trust and respect without guarantees of outcome. This trust includes the pain of integration needed to shift from reflexive polarization to the welcoming of difference.[12] These trends, both of distorting reality for security but also the rescuing, restorative work of CARE, are reflected in the left-hand page headings of each chapter. These often elusive tendencies deserve prominent notation in these efforts to illuminate the forces which shape our various levels of experience.

Notes

1 Solms (2013).
2 *Ibid.*
3 *The Telegraph* (2018).
4 Naar (2013).
5 Mackintosh (2017).
6 Hunt & Wheeler (2018).
7 Solana & Talbott (2016).
8 Hunt & Wheeler (2018).
9 A considered discussion of white working-class sentiment is offered by Berkeley Sociologist Arlie Hochschild in her book *Strangers in Their Own Land: Anger and Mourning on the American Right* (2016). In addition, a sensitive example of the white factory worker being overlooked by the export of jobs and industries can be found in the following podcast: Barbaro (2017a). As well, see a compelling account of the American move to the left under Obama's tenure at Beinart (2016).
10 Anderson, C. (2016).
11 Ellis (2017); Smith (2017); Oppenheim (2017).
12 Anderson, C. (2016), pp. 161–164; Anderson, M. (2016), chapters 6, 7; pp. 97–122.

PART I

The mind may distort reality in order to maintain security and stability

1

THE MYTH OF WHITE SUPREMACY

A myth that perpetuates an intense polarization amidst hatred occurred in Charlottesville, Virginia, on Friday August 11 and Saturday, August 12, 2017. A "Unite the Right" rally was held that weekend as a protest against the city-planned shrouding of the monument to the Confederate General Robert E. Lee. It was reported to be extensively planned with the needed permissions from city officials. On Friday evening a contingent of neo-Nazi and white supremacists conducted a torch-lit parade on the campus of the University of Virginia chanting among other Nazi slogans "Jews will not replace us."[1] This explicit reference to Nazi attitudes, so deadly during World War II, shocked many observers and may have stirred the vehemence of counter-protestors the next day. On Saturday morning, a cadre of white supremacist protestors marched toward Emancipation Park, the site of the Lee statue, and encountered agitated counter-protestors. Violent clashes between them began about 10:30 a.m. Just who began the violence is unclear, each side accusing the other. But the violence escalated rapidly until the Governor of Virginia declared a State of Emergency just after 11 a.m. Police seemed to be slow in responding to the violence, perhaps following criticism from Klan members for having enthusiastically intervened in a Ku Klux Klan rally previously.[2]

At 1:40 p.m. on Saturday afternoon a car sped into a group of marching counter-protestors, injuring nineteen and killing one. The driver of the car was charged with second degree murder and held without bail. News media and private videos reveal violent outbursts instigated by individuals on each side. Apparently, several white supremacist groups from around the U.S. and Europe had participated in the rally.[3] This electrified a nation that had thought that neo-Nazi activity and overt racism had significantly receded in recent decades. Several investigative reporters found that white supremacist organizations currently have significant activity and attraction, especially among young white men in contemporary America.[4]

President Donald Trump spoke to reporters on the Saturday afternoon, condemning "hatred, bigotry, and violence on many sides." His failure to condemn the neo-Nazis and white supremacists shocked many, as U.S. presidents have for decades actively condemned these movements. A day later Trump condemned these groups but on the following Tuesday he once again spoke of violence on the left, seeming to erase his delayed condemnation of the white nationalist organizations.[5] Several pro-right news commentators echoed that literally Trump was speaking a truth: that violence was perpetrated by both sides. Left-leaning media cited the Friday night provocations, the neo-Nazi display ("Jews will not replace us"), feeling that such a demonstration that was not countered by an explicit condemnation of such white racism was the real issue.[6] Several corporate heads then resigned from the president's American Manufacturing Council in protest for his seemingly siding with white nationalist organizations, a move which precipitated the demise of this advisory council.[7]

Then, on Wednesday evening a large gathering of faculty and students at the University of Virginia, in order to reclaim the ground that the white supremacists had marched over the previous weekend, held a candle-lit march on campus to "take back the Lawn."[8]

And the following Saturday, August 19, a week after the initial events, a rally of the alt-right, which was scheduled to meet in a portion of Boston Common, was massively overwhelmed by approximately 30,000 counter-protestors who took over the Common, far out-matching the rally in numbers and voices.[9] The rally ended sooner than scheduled because the speakers could not be heard.

This brief overview of the protest and counter-protest revolving around white supremacy in the summer of 2017, what has come to be called "Charlottesville", demonstrates several issues:

- One being how robust the white supremacy movement is in America today; another is the intensity of the divisiveness which this movement still triggers.

- As well, how ancestral hatreds die hard. Most Americans had hoped that the Nazi era was extinguished as the world recovered from World War II. The nation has been shocked to see how the neo-Nazi spirit dwells robustly amidst the white supremacy movement.
- Individual citizens may also be startled by their seeming unawareness, and, perhaps, by their denial of a simmering hatred and the wish to provocatively express that hatred by violence and intimidation.

A closer look requires focusing on three issues which have polarized Americans for centuries: black slavery in North America, a Southern code of honor, and the Civil War (1861–1865). The institution of slavery had been an integral part of several southern colonies ever since their founding in the 17th century.[10] Following the American Revolution (1775–1781), these colonies, now states, retained slave-based agricultural economies as crucial for their continued existence. Shame-based honor, the sense of self-worth based on how one feels viewed by others, played a pivotal role in sustaining the identity of the Southern planter class, fostering the myth of a genteel, leisurely, benevolent society. Its significance will be apparent throughout the text.

Indeed, the framers of the U.S. Constitution, many of whom were slave-holding planters from powerful Southern states, likely adhered to this code of honor. In any event, they could not in their lifetimes re-solve the question of slavery and its containment nor its spread within new territories and states as the country grew. Nor could the issue be settled during the next seventy-five years as voices of abolition grew in the North, while the Southern states ardently held to their right to maintain their personal property, that is, slaves. In the 1850s, a decade before the Civil War began, it is estimated that the value of the slaves held in the South was nearly equal to the value of the land, so that economic pressure toward continuing slavery was great.[11]

In order to dampen the growing restiveness in the South, the U.S. Congress attempted to achieve compromises in terms of the proportion of slave-holding and slave-free states. But a retrospective view suggests that the Civil War was inevitable. The Old (pre-war) South had, over generations, become beholden to slavery as the basis for its economy and its culture. In addition, it was far more oriented to the rights of the various states to determine their own destinies than the North's decided preference to retain the union of the states as primary. And significantly, the South had come to feel that its very identity was being threatened by Northern pressures regarding the abolition of slavery. So, the Southern slave states felt honor- and duty-bound to secede from the United States after the 1860 election of Abraham Lincoln.

Writing at least two books on the Southern concept of honor,[12] one of which was a finalist for the Pulitzer Prize,[13] Bertram Wyatt-Brown notes "The threat to slavery's legitimacy in the Union prompted the . . . secession crisis but it was Southern honor that pulled the trigger."[14] He offers a carefully considered view of Southern honor, variously described, as pivotal in the maintenance of the pre-war culture. He also describes in some detail, how the devastating loss of culture, land, and hopes for the future which followed the Civil War, had to be denied, distorted and channeled into visceral hatred, torment and blame of the now-freed black man and woman. Wyatt-Brown's discussions about shame-based honor offer some depth of understanding as to why there is such continuing sympathy for Confederate monuments, memorabilia and modern white supremacist movements. Keeping the flame of Southern honor alive, he suggests, maintains the un-mourned fable of white supremacy. It also shifts the blame for the war entirely on to the North's seeming tyrannical imposition of its culture on the South. From this view, then, shame-based honor also carries forward the assumption of gallantry, nobility and victimhood in its myth of the Lost Cause. Much of this book's understanding of Southern Honor and its legacy of an un-mourned myth relies on these works by Wyatt-Brown.

Even so, it is important to realize that not all Southerners were caught up in the myth or the distortions which shame-based honor would bestow. Many, grounded in whole-minded thought, whether in post-bellum or contemporary eras, would have appreciated the more complex realities involving layering of emotions, cultural forces, racial difference, emotional attachment and indeed the uncertainties which clear-eyed attention brings. The use of "Southern honor" and similar terms throughout this book is meant more as a short-hand term for the state of mind sculpted by loyalty to the myth and its defense than a broad reference to all Southerners. My emphasis on the forces that erode the mind may seem at times to minimize this recognition.

President Lincoln's Emancipation Proclamation (1862) began the process of freeing the slaves in the American South, but for many white Southerners, such a proclamation could have only enflamed the outrage that triggered the secessionist activities.[15] According to several historians[16] in the Old South, among the wealthy white population, there appeared to have developed a rather romantic view of Southern gentility and leisure, based on this appearance-based code of honor, to which many white Southerners subscribed: wealthy whites living out the life of apparent gentility while poor white Southerners felt caught up in the promise of trickle-down benefits from such wealth and leisure.[17]

The defeat of the Old South in 1865, of course, was devastating, not only to the slave economy, but to the white Southern sense of identity and way of life. Several historians suggest that the pivotal, often unspoken, element in this cultural illusion was that keeping blacks as an underclass, "keeping them in their place" would maintain the whites, both the planter class and the poor white farmer, in their securely "superior" position.[18]

From the view of this book, this myth of white superiority is based on the mental mechanisms of splitting and projection. Splitting and projection are early and universal mental mechanisms that seem to cleave the mind from its capacity for reflexive thought, rendering it back to the less complex state which only perceives absolutes, such as "good and bad" and "how things are." This reversion to a concrete view of reality may occur when doubt, pain or uncertainty are too much to bear. In these circumstances the mind is attracted to unquestionable certainties and anything felt to otherwise, such as doubt, is expelled and then perceived to reside or define a "bad or denigrated other." Thus, the mind *splits* off its own doubted aspects, and by *projection* attributes them to others. Myths, such as the myth of white supremacy, may be elaborated to bolster these attributions of goodness to the self and badness to the other.

But the seeming riddance actually creates a sense of underlying danger on at least three counts: the self feels diminished due to a portion of it having been split off and projected; and that unacceptable part is now felt to be an ever-hovering external enemy. In addition, the violence introduced by the mechanism of splitting only heightens the general sense of endangerment. This early mode of would-be protection, then, entraps one in a survival mentality characterized by tribal states (us and them, good and bad) and entrenched polarized positions. Without a wider sense of clear-eyed thought this sense of danger only escalates and continues the entrapment in polarization, absolutism, fear and hatred. These mechanisms may, then, imprison not only the personality but a culture over time. As well, in the absence of clear thought as an antidote, power-based functioning, such as tyranny, can flourish to the detriment of communities and indeed nations. Understanding these entrapments and the sources for rescue are major themes in this book. The consequences of these polarizing defenses along with the bolstering myths have been well described by the Southern writer W. J. Cash in his book *The Mind of the South*.[19] Much of his book outlines various aspects of this maintenance of the myth of white superiority amidst a fragile interior.

Cash suggests, rather bluntly, how the white Southern mind, in viewing a society based on slavery as genteel and benevolent, was also enslaved. Such a view, he suggests, rested on maintaining a static, unquestioning society based on appearance and manners, where active discussion of the reality of slavery could not occur. In fact, Cash says, that doing so would have been tantamount to heresy or treason. The real underpinning of its culture and economy, that is, the harsh emotional costs of slavery, could be more noted by contemporary non-Southern observers. This may be seen in the diaries of William (known as Henry) and Frances Seward, native New Yorkers, in their tour of the South in the summer of 1835.[20]

It should be noted that many wealthy families in Northern states owned slaves during and after the American Revolution (1776–1781). But, according to historian Wyatt-Brown, by the 1830s, these states were turning more toward internal (guilt) rather than external (shame) measures of self-worth.[21] Such internal scrutiny fostered learning from one's experiences, thus fostering growth and change. These factors likely played a part in Northerners increasingly embracing abolition, New York having eradicated slavery in 1827. Thus, according to this view, they were not as caught up in the myth that was freezing views in the Southern states. Henry Seward, born into a wealthy New York slave-owning family in 1801, had several childhood playmates who had been born into slavery in his and neighboring families. His growing abolitionist sentiments likely stemmed from his feeling disturbed to see the situation to which some of these black playmates were subject.[22] By 1835, then, when he and his young family were touring Virginia, his (and likely his wife's) views were influenced by abolitionist leanings. While the trip through Pennsylvania and into Virginia was planned as a get-away from the pressures of Seward's growing law practice, their impressions must have re-focused their attention, at least in part, on slavery issues which had so long occupied public conversation in the North.

Historian Doris Kearns Goodwin cites the Seward letters and diary entries of that intended trip which reveal their personal observations and emotional impressions.[23] One strong impression upon crossing into Virginia was of a static world, seemingly unchanged for decades. Henry Seward bemoaned "a waste(d), broken tract of land . . . with old, decaying habitation . . . How deeply the curse of slavery is set upon this venerated . . . region of the old dominion."[24] They observed both the land and the people to be stagnant and neglected, with none of the signs of vigor and upward mobility they were used to seeing and feeling among their Northern neighbors.

Seward's wife, Frances, wrote of families fragmented by children being sold to distant plantations. She and Henry were deeply moved at the sight of several black children tied together in a string, as one might arrange beasts of burden being driven to market, all tethered to a white man, with rope and whip, who was taking them to the auction block in Richmond.[25] This sight and its emotional impact led the Sewards to cut short their journey and return to the North. Their emotional state might be summarized by what Frances wrote in her journal: "sick of slavery and the South . . . the evil effects constantly coming before me and marring everything."[26] This Northern view, experienced some twenty-five years before the Civil War, could observe more of the reality of stasis, neglect and cruelty which the myth of white supremacy had to mask for those white Southern citizens dependent on the slave-based economy for their livelihood and sense of belonging.

The Seward diaries of the 1830s, then, echo the laments of Cash written a century later. In an atmosphere shaped by the myth of white supremacy the mind could not be open to viewing disturbing realities, or for growth via questioning, nor to the welcoming of new ideas. Cash's notations would support this understanding as he describes the Southern focus on surfaces, appearances and action rather than toward considered thought.

Human nature, of course, is complex, and Alexis de Tocqueville's observations, in 1831, of the Northern attitudes toward freed blacks, may be helpful, while initially confusing. This curious French observer of American life, who traveled extensively in America during that year was astonished to observe significant racial prejudice toward black freedmen in the North and the western part of America at that time. His conclusion was that parts of America that were not slave-holding were more prejudiced than those that were slave-holding.[27] We might feel puzzled by and initially question these observations, until we consider the function of the psychic mechanisms of splitting and projection: in the 1830s abolitionist views were growing in the North, but this does not rule out the function of the Northern citizens attributing their prejudice to the slave-holding South, thus feeling free of those troubling sentiments. Conscious denial of prejudice does not preclude unconscious or denied prejudice from functioning; one can say one thing even to oneself, but act in ways which betray deeply held, although denied, feelings and fears. We will return to racial prejudice across America in later parts of the book. For now, we will return to considerations of historians' views of the Southern experience.

For many Southerners, the election of Abraham Lincoln, in 1860, seemed to be the last straw. The Old South saw him as an anti-slavery President, offering unbearable insult to the South's way of life. The slave states of the South then seceded to preserve their way of life; but they also seceded, according to Cash, to preserve this static, blinkered state of mind. He says the self-consciousness of the Southern view was strengthened during the Civil War, in terms of the romantic notions of the heroism of fighting the good fight and being overrun by numbers. This perspective, known as the Lost Cause, became a way to view the War and Southern defeat in the somewhat romantic light where honor remained in central focus, all responsibility for impulsiveness and belligerence ascribed elsewhere. Subsequent violence, seen as defending the honor of the South, including that which would reinstate white supremacy, was nearly always considered to be patriotic.

Historian Wyatt-Brown[28] describes the Lost Cause myth in the following way:

> Out of the weakness that military and racial overthrow had created in 1865, Southern whites gradually constructed a fabric of nostalgia for the Lost Cause. When coupled with the notion of 'Redemption' from allegedly evil Republican and black rule, this means of interpreting the late war offered the concept of victimization, (rather than) abject military defeat. Like the Japanese in the years since the fall of their empire in 1945, white Southerners accepted no blame for oppression against weaker people. In fact, denial was uppermost as it had been for the first generation of Germans in acknowledging culpability for the Nazi Holocaust. For most whites, slavery may have been economically deficient, but, most everyone agreed, owners had largely been magnanimous, scrupulous, loving, and responsible in their rule. Yankee skullduggery, not Southern impulsiveness, had brought on the great conflict. (p. 282)

The degree of splitting and projection required to achieve these revisionist views of the war, and to offer protection from appreciating stark realities, may be apparent.

But, for balance, a remarkable interview with the leader of the Confederacy, Jefferson Davis, deserves inclusion. It illustrates the intensity of the Southern view, which considered the North as imposing a tyranny that must be fought to the last man. This interview appeared in the *Atlantic Monthly*[29] in 1864, penned by James Gilmore, a private citizen from the North who, seeing that the South was losing badly, sought to explore the possibility for peace negotiations with influential Southern leaders. His interview with Davis was noted in detail at the time and the following are quotes from the article. When asked whether peace talks could ensue, Davis emphatically said only if the North granted independence, that is, agreeing for the Southern states to secede from the Union. Setting the issue of slavery to the side, emphasizing self-rule, Davis said:

> The North was mad and blind; it would not let us govern ourselves; and so, the war came, and now it must go on till the last man of this generation falls in his tracks, and his children seize his musket and fight his battle, *unless you acknowledge our right to self-government.* We are not fighting for slavery. We are fighting for Independence—and that, or extermination, we *will* have it. (pp. 349–350, emphasis in the original)

A bit further in this interview Davis was quoted as saying:

> if our whole country were devastated, and our armies crushed and disbanded, – could we, without giving up our manhood, give up our right to govern ourselves? Would you not rather die, and feel yourself a man than live, and be subject to a foreign power? (pp. 355–356)

Gilmore noted the galvanizing quality of Davis' presentation, and how with this man at the helm in the South, the War would likely have to be fought to the bitter end. Inclusion of this point of view helps us to appreciate the complexity of emotions in the South and toward the South. Different emphases trigger passionate polarizations: at this late point in the War, the South felt urgent about the right of self-government, but more basically it appears, from Davis' comments, that they felt the sense of Southern pride and potency to be severely threatened. The Northern view stressed the abolition of slavery and re-union of all the states. And, as we will continue to note, polarized positions can only demonize the opposition. While, from the distance of 160 years we might be able to hold both positions in mind, we might also appreciate that, at the time, such polarized views must have created a seemingly unbridgeable divide.

Following the War, from the view of many Southerners, the Northern impositions during Reconstruction—land taken from planters and given to the former slaves, education and voting privileges for these new citizens, efforts toward equality—continued the degradations of Southern identity.

This Southern sentiment, as a bitter lament, is vividly expressed in the 1864 diary entry of a young school teacher who was emigrating from slave-state Missouri to war-free Montana Territory. The diary entry reads:

> In this time of war and desolation we read daily accounts of human suffering inflicted by human hand(s). (A) wicked ruler is said to be the greatest scourge that can be visited on a nation . . . The war which at first claimed to be one to restore the union has progressed steadily (;) now the avowed object is to emancipate the slaves and make the negro the equal of the white man or rather degrade the white man to the level of the negro. What startling evidences this war has given of human depravity.[30]

Again, the unbridgeable divide: for this Southern view, the depravity was seen as Lincoln's effort to pull the white man down. From the Northern view, the effort was to lift the black man up, while re-uniting the states and peoples. The intensity of the Southern view as cited in various references—having one's honor and whole way of being degraded—would become an unquenchable hatred, to be carried through with vehemence and violence to the present because the reality of the loss of the Old South could not be faced and mourned. And thus the view of having been degraded by a hateful other (the North) could not be resolved through a sense of re-unification. And, consequently, the myth of white supremacy could not then, and for many, cannot even now, be easily surrendered.

We cannot know whether Lincoln's intended plans for reconciliation of Southern states back into the Union might have gone better if he had survived the assassin's bullet; that is, whether his presence and personal role in management might have maintained mutual respect during this enormous Southern upheaval. What we do know is that many white Southerners seemed to experience Northern efforts to elevate the blacks as deliberately degrading the white Southerner. Indeed, many Northerners, known as carpetbaggers, did go into the South to manipulate and exploit the decimated society for their own profit, another source of hatred for Southern whites. Still, Cash and Wyatt-Brown suggest that the white Southern self-respect built on shame-based honor, appearance and myth, so erased by defeat at the end of the Civil War, left many white Southerners feeling they must turn to violent action as a patriotic duty.[31] As soon as the North withdrew its forces and its will toward Reconstruction (1865–1877) violence especially toward the black citizenry began.

Wyatt-Brown[32] offers further detail:

> The honor of (the white Southern) family and community was involved . . . and to shy away . . . was to show a cowardly spirit. Both (duel and lynching) were supposed to have a vindicating and cleansing effect so that community members could return to their usual pursuits, happy in the thought that somehow a balance of nature had been restored. Photographs of white crowds stolidly and unashamedly facing the camera with a black body dangling from a nearby tree limb reveal their collective sense of having done a righteous and honorable deed. (p. 284)

Southern vigilantes carried on these 'values' of honor, and the sacredness of white womanhood. And whole communities sanctioned such killings. Wyatt-Brown suggests, as do others, that many white Southerners could neither fathom nor process the absolute loss of their pre-War way of life. Nor could they relinquish the ethic and myth of the white Southern planter class, that is, the natural assumption of the black underclass. The resurgence of white supremacy, then, was for many a way to keep this assumption alive. Its support by the white community in the South suggests, indeed, that this assumption was held more or less as a conviction, not only by veterans of the war, but by much of the white community at large.

The vehemence of this position, including the view of the North as tyrannically imposing its values, further degrading the Southern way of life, offers some context, aside from the complex issue of slavery, for the seemingly intransigent hatred many Southerners have carried down the generations toward the North (and federal issues).

The sense of this aspect of white Southern identity, then, may be considered before the Civil War to have rested in firmly held but unspoken ways of maintaining honor by bolstering a myth via black enslavement. Subsequent to the War, much of Southern identity apparently also incorporated a perpetual resistance and hatred of all things relating to the North and its offerings.[33] Cash notes that this unquenchable hatred of Northern views further crippled the poor Southern white, in that the opportunity to learn to read and write, brought by Northern teachers during Reconstruction, an offering so readily accepted by the freed slaves, was resisted by poor Southern whites who felt it to be another Northern imposition, perhaps even Northern brain-washing.[34]

We are noting how hatred itself hobbles the mind, congealing it in bitterness, suspicion, envy and fear, such that any benevolent offerings are experienced only as humiliating or suspicious intrusions. We can surmise that it would have seemed like a betrayal of Southern group values to accept any largesse, such as education, from the federal government. As these attitudes have come down the generations, this recognition may explain to some degree current-day hatred and resistance toward federal government benefits.[35] To those feeling loyal to the legacy of the Southern hatred of the North, appreciating such federally provided benefits as social security or health care might feel disloyal to the spirit of Southern pride and resistance.

Cash notes that the Yankee efforts to "wean the South from its divergences and to bring it into the flow of the nation, which . . . was the most fundamental drive behind the Yankee's behavior"[36] only strengthened the white Southern resolve, intensely held by some, to remain master over the black man. And *this* civil war, that is, maintaining the Southern separateness and keeping the black man subservient, so opposite to what the North had wished to establish, Cash maintains, the ardent Southerner won. ". . . it was this Yankee's fate to have strengthened it (the entrenched Southern state of mind) almost beyond reckoning, and to have made it one of the most solidly established, one of the least *reconstructible*[37] (states of mind) ever developed"[38] (emphasis in the original).

Cash's book was published in 1941, but his formulation foretold the continuing Southern resistance and hatred emergent even in the 1960s toward federal efforts through the courts to equalize education and protect civil and voting rights for blacks. Such actions, begun 100 years previously during Reconstruction, had been met with ongoing intransigence and brutality by Southern municipalities and states. While Cash's point of view may be one of the most pessimistic of the historians writing about the post-War South,[39] his view may accurately plumb the core of hatred, based on fantasy, fear, and revenge, which has primed the Southern white supremacy movement for hundreds of years. This is a major reason why as a historian of this era he is cited here.

The different ethical bases shaping attitudes in the North and the South may be important to consider in terms of significant misunderstandings which lead to such polarization. The North, whose ethics by the mid-1800s were shaped mostly by guilt,[40] that is, the capacity for internal discourse with oneself about right and wrong, felt that the South would be similarly moved by remorse about slavery and its brutalities. Northerners apparently had not anticipated the degree of hatred and enmity which were fueled by the South's sense of shame-based honor that could only feel abject humiliation in defeat. Common ground based on respect for self and other could not be found as the South's honor had its foundation on shame and humiliation, win or lose. It could only regain its honor by defeating the goals of the Northern victors. Entrenched revenge for defiled honor seemed to be intensely felt by many in the South for more than a century.

Research for this book has revealed how enriching various authors' views may be about a complex and enigmatic subject, such as the enduring Southern myth of white supremacy. It has thus felt most respectful to present, as possible, each perspective. Interwoven into this discussion will be a psychoanalytic view of some of the observations these authors offer.

The first view comes from a recent book by Berkeley sociologist Arlie Russell Hochschild, *Strangers in their own Land*. She describes her visits over a ten-year period with several ardent Tea Party voters in Louisiana. Through her patient, candid discussions she got to know the influences and motivations of these Southern working-class voters. She came to realize that their over-riding view of government as too big and too intrusive appeared to be an echo of the North intruding upon Southern freedom (once again) with regulations. The 'once again' refers to the North's imposition of re-union and Reconstruction upon the defeated and thus humiliated South. Hochschild's impression is that this deep wound, as ongoing humiliation, has never really healed. The seeming disconnect for a Northern observer of the welcoming of polluting industry into one's neighborhood can be understood when one realizes that, for these modern-day workers, big industry brings back the image of the Southern planter class with its seeming largess and trickle-down benevolence. The enduring romantic notion of the Southern aristocracy, with its generosity and its benevolence toward all whites, is apparent. Less spoken, but clearly significant, as well, is the myth of white supremacy for the self-esteem of these Louisianans. As long as there is a black underclass, this myth presumes, the white working class can feel respect-worthy.

Hochschild also notes how Southern white working-class values differ from liberal coastal values. She describes the values of tradition, endurance, sacrifice, and pride of place. These values, which honor continuity, tradition and self-reliance, prompt these citizens to consider federal support for minorities, such as blacks and refugees, as tantamount to letting them cut ahead of these Southern workers in their decades-long wait to move up the social ladder toward the American Dream. Resentment then abounds toward liberal government policies as well as the beneficiaries of those programs. In addition, jobs, rather than the environment, feel vital to the Southern worker. Big business, primarily oil, reminds them of the tradition of benevolent paternalism, said to be a legacy of the antebellum past. In gratitude, these workers excuse any pollution which accompanies this major local employer.

Another significant source, Carole Anderson's book *White Rage: The Unspoken Truth of our Racial Divide*, relays how resistant even non-Southern white society seems to be to black advancement. Echoing de Tocqueville's observation, she suggests that white supremacy was not just an attitude in the American South. While, during the 20th Century, Northern cities have offered jobs with better pay, integration within communities, schools, and housing has been very contentious in many cities and states across the nation. She feels there is a wide consensus among whites that black advancement somehow threatens white Americans' own prosperity. Programs which have privileged disadvantaged minorities are felt as taking something away from white Americans, the stance noted also by Hochschild in her understanding of the contemporary white Southern working class.

This theme of ongoing white resentment is echoed in Michelle Alexander's book *The New Jim Crow*, in which she vividly describes how the pressures to keep the black man down have continued in the past few decades by way of mass incarceration of young black and brown men, under the guise of the War on Drugs. More recently, she suggests, unwarranted police brutalities and lethal assaults on young black men have continued this policy. Alexander presents compelling evidence of the continuance of white subjugation of blacks, almost unremittingly, since the civil rights legislation of the 1960s. The current incarceration of young black men seems to her to reveal a picture of warehousing them in prisons as if to erase them from relevance.

With an eye to hatred in the contemporary American political scene, Carole Anderson notes that the election of Barack Obama triggered significant hatred, perhaps because of some of his successes as president. Republicans, and specifically Tea Party members, from her view, seemed to do nothing but try to obstruct his policies and maneuver voting regulations.

> The vitriol heaped on Obama was simply unprecedented—not least given the sheer scale of challenges he found himself confronting and the measurable success he achieved in doing so . . . Obama's centrist solutions and utter lack of radicalism in the face of a recalcitrant and obstructionist Congress should have made him a hero to traditional Republicans. But just the opposite happened; by the end if his first term the president had an 85.7 percent *disapproval* rating among the GOP. One progressive wrote, "You hate Obama with a passion, despite the fact that he is a tax cutting, deficit reducing war President

who undermines civil rights and delivers corporate friendly watered-down reforms that benefit special interests just like a Republican. You call him a Kenyan. You call him a socialist. You dance with your hatred. . . . (emphasis added)[41]

Obama received death threats and expressions of hatred far surpassing the experience of other presidents.

Somehow, many have convinced themselves that the man who pulled the United States back into some semblance of financial health, reduced unemployment to its lowest level in decades, secured health insurance for millions of citizens, ended one of our recent, all-too-intractable wars in the Middle East, reduced the staggering deficit he inherited from George W. Bush, and masterminded the takedown of Osama bin Laden actually hates America.[42]

Anderson holds that instead of pride in the progress of America, in terms of the nation being able to celebrate the election of a black man, around the country communities of black persons felt a chilling sense of physical vulnerability, not so different from the intimidating threats of lynching in the post-Reconstruction era. Instead of progress, the achievements of a black president seemed to be experienced by many as a direct threat; his success, perhaps being felt as "taking over the country."[43]

An important psychological element to understand about intense hatred is how intimately it is linked to fear, both in the hated ones (blacks fearful when Obama was elected) but also within the hating ones in terms of the expectation of retaliation ('take over the country'). The riots in Charlottesville and the neo-Nazi chant "Jews will not replace us" mentioned earlier in this chapter, echo this intimate link between hate and fear. The inevitable link between hatred and fear will be further explored later in this chapter.

Nancy Isenberg's recent book *White Trash: 400 Years of the Untold Story of Class in America* discusses the long-existing and long-denied presence of dispossessed peoples, the seeming dregs of European cities, virtually dumped on Eastern North American shores for 400 years beginning in the 1600s. These marginalized people have moved slowly into the American South but have remained relatively unintegrated into American society or the American psyche. Examples include the hillbillies of Appalachia and poor white farmers who have been squeezed into marginal farming lands in the South for generations.[44]

One conclusion from this book might be a meditation on the dispossessed and how we cleave away our awareness of their existence and their plight; we blame them for their poverty, as if they had a choice to live in other than the poorest conditions. We deny them as our ancestors and refuse to see our own tendencies to push them away from desired lands or opportunities, but also from our own minds. We split off our awareness and our knowledge. And they, having felt our rejection of them, now resist our latter-day efforts to aid them, feeling (rather correctly) that we are only looking down on them.

Edward Ayers, a contemporary historian of the American South and of the Civil War, demonstrates in detail how attitudes changed rapidly with the approach of the War. He cites neighboring towns, just a few miles apart, on either side of the Mason-Dixon Line, the traditional demarcation between the North and the South. Newspaper reports about each other's town, previously amicable in nature, became shrill and sharp in tone and violent in language as war seemed closer. Positions hardened, former friends became foes: "the misguided frenzy and folly and madness of your people (that has caused the war)" cries out the newspaper on the south side of the Mason-Dixon Line toward its neighbor. The Southern paper continues to rant that the Northern town is "craven and cheap . . . bigoted . . . and tightfisted . . . refuge of the vagabond." Whereas its own side is the "flower of southern honor and chivalry."[45] The Northern paper replied in kind.

The violence of the language quoted is noteworthy: "misguided frenzy and folly and madness . . ." are phrases which may be seen as expressing the shards of a splintered personality; equally it is the language of attack. The violence expressed may be thought of as evidence of the violence of the splitting which fear brings about. The language is not only violent, but polarizing as well, in terms of your "misguided frenzy" but "our brave and gallant sons."

Ayers also allows glimpses of what violence and war (external or internal) may achieve. Regarding righteousness "The secret of the Civil war was that many Americans . . . wanted to prove their patriotism and demonstrate that they held God's favor."[46]

> Regarding the power of violence and polarization to redefine personal identities, former friends easily became foes. The Civil War . . . demonstrated . . . the power of . . . (polarized positions) . . . to define people's understanding of themselves. It demonstrated the ability of war and violence to recast identities, to submerge the self in the thrill of tribal belonging.[47]

The complexities of various contingencies allow better appreciation of how inter-dependent everyday realities of history may become. Noting this, we may realize how much we crave simplicity. It is wearying to hold in mind the awareness of ever-shifting events that comprise the reality about issues of the day. When we wish to become clear about a complex issue, such as hatred, we generally simplify it, often reducing it to black and white terms.[48]

As well, hatred itself narrows our view, and excites our passions, as Ayers suggests. These trends tend to impede balanced thought. We may slip into condemnation of one side or another. Further thought suggests that when we simplify things we may get excited, as if we are seeing things more clearly, or are closer to the truth. We also may adhere more tightly to a similar-thinking group, to bolster our newly found "certainties." Durkheim describes sharing a level of excitement as "collective effervescence."[49] Ayers also suggests this in his comment "to submerge the self in the thrill of tribal belonging" (p. 413).

Hatred in this chapter is viewed as a product of the violence of the processes of splitting and projection. Hatred may also be thought of as a strong tie to a person who is the recipient of the projections of one's own hated qualities. As Ayers' examples assert, when hatred sets in attitudes become hardened and narrow, giving way to the sharded world of hate and fear. As polarities develop, the hated one is seen as "your misguided frenzy," and one's self and family as "our brave and gallant sons." We can easily substitute similar polarized comments in contemporary American political discussions, probably more accurately described as harangue rather than discourse or dialogue. We can also note how leadership sets the tone, whether guided by mutual respect or by the incitement to disruptive thought and action.

The resulting polarization involves the mind's reversion to black and white thinking. Contempt may then be considered as a defense against the shame which is incumbent in the descent from whole-minded thought.[50] This view holds that in order to avoid the pain of one's own shame, it may be projected to then allow one to look down from a position of contempt upon the recipient of that projected shame. Many Southerners, prior to the Civil War, may have felt contempt toward the North's apparent lack of cultural elegance, mocking its grimy industries and thirst for money. They may then have felt threatened at the end of the war by the fantasy of becoming objects of contempt in the eyes of the victorious North. Such fantasies, extremely painful in any culture, may have in part fueled the retaliatory lynchings in parts of the South. Similar fantasies of contempt may have prompted the continuing brutality and belittlement of blacks.[51] Similar fears may also fuel the extraordinary polarization in contemporary American politics, where bi-partisan dialogue is often considered weakness or capitulation. Looking closely at the consequences of splitting and projection allows us to see how the descent of the mind may lead to brutal reactivity, just as it likely fostered vicious atrocities in earlier times.

A few words about the modern concept of evil seem warranted. Manifestations of hatred involve active personages—the hater and the hated. The attribution of evil, however, seems to involve the dehumanization of all parties, via dissociation from any moral agency. The resulting fracture of the self and loss of humanity renders the one attributed as an evil-doer as barely human, without ethical or moral constraint. This figure, then, may be seen, indeed, may be felt as capable of numbly and mindlessly committing all manner of atrocities without compunction. Such a robotic murdering machine may be seen to arise especially when there is a felt pressure from peers, or the now-authoritarian other. Examples from the Nazi era come easily to mind. Also, to most modern observers the lynchings in the post-Reconstruction South may be considered to carry the attribution of evil deeds. They were ostensibly carried out to avenge and thus to redeem the shame-based honor of the Old South. The excitement and seeming pride in the faces of the whites in photos of lynchings suggest that they were indeed pleased to be recorded as participants in these acts. So, they were obviously not considering that they were participating in evil. But then, neither did the Nazis, who were consciously bent on clearing away the subhuman rubbish from Europe.

Arendt, Covington and others[52] emphasize that the would-be evil-doer appears to not have access to enlivenment by a care-bringing other. The concept of evil, from a modern view, may then be considered more as involving states of mind which are accessible when one has abandoned or been coerced away from one's own humanity. Such allows consideration of evil deeds rather than evil people.

And finally, a few thoughts about the power of intense negative affect to define the reality of both the active and the passive parties. Just as maternal reverie ties the mother with loving affect to the infant in her receiving and metabolizing the infant's distress, both the hating and the hated parties are bound in a field of hate. If there were no binding between the two participants, the hater's hatred, lacking a target, would be dispersed into unbounded space and he or she would feel destabilized and debilitated. James Baldwin, in his 1965 Cambridge debate[53] exemplifies this strong tie in his description of the white Southern sheriff who cannot fathom why the black man whose identity is so (negatively) bound up by the same culture as his, would wish to complain or leave. Baldwin suggests that the sheriff cannot imagine this tension-ridden relationship being disturbed by either party, as such would disturb the generations of dominance-subservience which, while asymmetric and often brutal, offered continuity.

Carole Anderson notes[54] the extraordinary means Southern whites used to keep black workers from leaving the South to flee the atrocities of lynching and other terrors that whites had been perpetrating since the 1870s. A close reading of that portion of her book suggests that there were desperate attempts to keep the black objects of their hatred from being able to leave, likely to both retain control over them, as well as to have familiar targets for their hatred and venom.

The recipient of the projected shame feels bound by the powerful unconscious pressure to feel penetrated by the projected affect. A quotation, from the early black activist Frederick Douglass, writing in 1853, describes this burden of received contempt.

> The great mass of American citizens estimates us (blacks) as being a characterless and purposeless people, and hence we hold up our heads, if at all, against the withering influence of a nation's scorn and contempt.[55]

The recipient of projected shame, then, may feel insistently drawn to respond as if defined by the shame and thus act in ways which appear to warrant the contempt evident in the projector. The legacy of such penetrating shame can cascade down the generations and may seem to define a people (the blacks) 160 years after Emancipation. It seems to take more generations to rectify this imbalance and to realize that the shame should actually reside in those aggressively carrying forward the myth of white supremacy.

Some psychoanalysts call this powerful emotional interplay projective identification. But this technical phrase may be overly cumbersome for nimble understanding of this emotional dance as an active to and fro between projector and recipient of the projection.

These usually unconscious forces likely evolved prior to language as vehicles to convey or manage emotion. Just as in the herd, groups can feel the ripple-through effect of intense emotion as communal experience. To be the hub of intense projection may be a rather strange experience. Being drawn into foreign thoughts, feelings and actions can be very compelling.[56] Fantasies and tales of being possessed by spirits, evil and otherwise, may derive from this phenomenon of being deeply penetrated by others' projected emotions. Indeed, it may feel like being caught in a mysterious gravitational field.

So, human experience indicates that emotions cannot be divorced from intellect. Moreover, thought about embattling emotions is difficult to attain. And consideration of intense polarizing emotions in a balanced way is a daunting task.

Historical and social psychology studies further illuminate the universality and consequences of splitting and projection. Still, it is difficult to confront the ubiquity of this process. In our normal growth and development choices are made when we affiliate with family and other intimates. In doing so, we exclude others, thereby creating a demarcation between those we choose to be with and those we do not. Tribal forces and legacies of evolution, of course, come into play here.[57] Recognition of such gives the widest possibility for appreciating the complexity of our human emotions. Such recognition may soften our experience of humiliation when we are brought face to face with our own tendencies to possess and to dispossess.

The tragedy of remaining locked into these fractured states of mind may be further illustrated by how W. J. Cash ended his life.[58] Cash appeared to be a thoughtful, rather than a physically active, Southerner. But he felt that he was a failure, beginning with not living up to his father's and family's hopes. He did not feel truly valued by others or himself. Unlike the action-oriented Southerner, he often felt plagued by, rather than disavowing of, his inner doubts. He appeared to feel haunted by these internal demeaning voices, likely a major source for his abiding melancholy.

Revealing rather than concealing the cruelty and falsity of the Southern myth of white supremacy, he may have felt that he was deeply betraying the Southern tradition that was a part of his being. Soon after he finished this book in 1940, deeply worried about the war in Europe, he became obsessed with the terror that Nazi assassins were out to get him. This unbearable dread shortly before his death may have been linked to fantasies that, in exposing the shame and guilt of the South, which he did with clarity and candor, he was to be persecuted, and to be assassinated himself. That is, exposing the unthinkable truths hidden by myth in his fantasy could only lead to violent retribution. This fantasy, an inner torment and conviction, may have propelled his suicide by hanging. While this detail is breath-taking to encounter, it is also a reminder of how deadly un-metabolized pains and dreads can be. Further, it may have taken this descent into terror to fully expose the underbelly of pain, despair, fracture, violence, paranoia—the consequences of splitting and projection, and unquenchable hatred—which so laced the Southern mind, not only in the pre-Civil War era but into the present as well.

So, we may painfully learn from Cash's account, about the deadly cleavage which can emanate from the splitting processes. What may be difficult to realize is that when we engage in splitting we inevitably identify with *both* poles of experience. That is, as both victim and perpetrator. My understanding of these processes suggests that the assassins in Cash's mind may have emerged from the split off violence not only from a disapproving family, but from a society from which he could not fully dissociate, one willing to violently insist on the myth of white supremacy. This view then suggests that when Cash exposed that myth with the publication of his book, the violent aspect which had plagued him as melancholy coalesced into the inner conviction about the Nazi assassins. This conviction, then, either drove him to assassinate himself or to escape the terrifying torment by suicide. In either case, the dreaded fantasy of assassins or their murderous intent, as unquenchable hatred, led him to kill himself.

This tragic example is compelling. Appreciating the potential violence incumbent in the splitting processes demonstrates how entrapping they may be. It also illuminates how important it is to understand the underpinnings for such entrenchment as the first step toward rescue from this situation. Avenues of rescue are often hard-won, when the individual or indeed the society has been steeped for generations in vicious polarization.

Notes

1 Spencer & Stolberg (2017).
2 Ellis (2017).
3 Singal (2017).
4 Barbaro (2017b); White (2018).
5 Thrush (2017).
6 Dubenko (2017).
7 Shabad (2017).
8 Newman & Suchak (2017).
9 BBC News (2017).
10 *Since their founding in the 17th Century*: James Baldwin in a famous debate with William F. Buckley held at Cambridge University in 1965, makes the point that white attitudes toward slavery existed in Europe prior to the establishment of the American colonies. British and French attitudes toward the peoples in their various colonies over several generations exemplify this trend. Baldwin (1965) In addition, several historians have aptly noted the cultural conditions which promoted white supremacy in North America: Wyatt-Brown (2001, 1982); Anderson, C. (2017); Isenberg (2016); Ayers (2003).

11 Deyle (2005). Wyatt-Brown (2002) suggests that the value of slave property was upwards of three billion dollars in this antebellum period.
12 Wyatt-Brown (1982, 2002).
13 Wyatt-Brown (1982).
14 *Ibid.*, p. 178.
15 Cash (1941); Ayers (2003).
16 Wyatt-Brown (1982, 2001), Cash (1941), Lumpkin (1991), Donald (1981).
17 *benefits from such wealth and leisure:* Cash (1941): "The very marrow of this tradition of the backcountry . . . of the feeling which was basic in the Southern situation, was a sort of immense kindliness and easiness . . . of men who have long lived together on the same general plane, who have common memories, and who are more or less conscious of the ties of blood . . . this kindliness and easiness were flowing over (to become) the famous Southern manner." (pp. 40–41.) And after the Civil War, the fantasy of white southern largesse continued as a model for a majority of white southern citizens (pp. 154–156).
18 *the whites in their securely "superior" place:* Cash (1941), Chapter 3; p. 105; pp. 337–339; Hochschild (2016), pp. 208–209; Anderson, C. (2016), pp. 34, 73, 80, 100; Wyatt-Brown (2002).
19 Cash (1941).
20 Goodwin (2005), pp. 77–78.
21 Wyatt-Brown (1982), pp. 19–22; p. 100 "The difference between conscience as part of honorable bearing and conscience as an inner voice of God might seem slight as far as the actual way gentlemen behaved . . . Nevertheless, (the internal voice) quite clearly has a more telling effect in encouraging moderation, sexual continence, repression of anger and postponement of desires, because guilt is a more internal and self-dependent mechanism than shame."
22 Goodwin (2005), p. 31.
23 *Ibid.*, pp. 77–78.
24 *Ibid.*, p. 77.
25 Seward (1877), *An Autobiography*, p. 271, also in Goodwin (2005), p. 78: "Ten naked little boys, between six and twelve years old, tied together, two and two, by their wrists, were all fastened to a long rope, and followed by a tall, gaunt white man, who, with his long lash, whipped up the sad and weary little procession, drove it to the horse-trough to drink and thence to a shed, where they lay down on the ground and sobbed and moaned themselves to sleep."
26 Goodwin (2005), p. 78.
27 De Tocqueville (1863): "On the contrary, the prejudice of race appears to be stronger in the states that have abolished slavery than in those where it still exists; and nowhere is it so intolerant as in those states where servitude has never been known."
28 Wyatt-Brown (2001).
29 Gilmore (1864).
30 Dickson, Mary Frances Warren "Mollie." (1864). Private diary of young Missouri schoolteacher, now at the Museum of the Rockies, Bozeman, Montana. She moved to Montana by steamboat and wagon train with her father and sister toward the end of the War. It should be noted that the tone of the lament also reflects the several losses she had experienced with the death of one brother,

perhaps as a casualty of the War, as well as her mother. And now, as she writes this entry she is anticipating the loss of her Missouri friends of a decade or more.

31 Cash (1941), pp. 94, 99; Wyatt-Brown (1982, 2001).

32 Wyatt-Brown (2001).

33 Cash (1941), Book II, chapter I "Of the Frontier the Yankee Made."

34 Cash (1941), pp. 171–174.

35 Hochschild (2016), pp. 67–69.

36 Cash (1941), p. 105.

37 Regarding Reconstruction (1865–1877) efforts following the Civil War, after which the federal government withdrew its troops and much of its efforts to leave vengeful white Southerners more or less free to re-exert efforts to re-subjugate the black population within its bounds. Some of the most vicious acts of brutality against blacks occurred in the 1870s and 1880s, likely as suppressed hatred and humiliations left over from the War were unchecked.

38 Cash (1941), p. 107.

39 Wyatt-Brown (1991), pp. vii–xxxviii.

40 Wyatt-Brown (2001), pp. 154–155.

41 Anderson, C. (2016), pp. 155–156, quoting "An Open Letter to the People Who Hate Obama More Than They Love America," *Daily Kos*, January 9, 2012.

42 Taylor (2010).

43 Anderson, C. (2016), p. 160. In this comment Carole Anderson may not be reflecting how polarized the electorate has become: Obama was either loved (by the left) or hated (by the right). Just as Donald Trump, reciprocally is hated by the left and loved by many on the right.

44 In addition to Isenberg's excellent description, the opening chapter "Of Time and Frontiers" in Cash (1941), echoes this little-recognized and much denied aspect of American history and culture.

45 Ayers (2003), p. 152.

46 *Ibid.*, p. 187.

47 *Ibid.*, p. 413.

48 Anderson, M. (2016), pp. 100, 101. For a discussion of how we simplify, even concretize concepts into things in order to try to understand them.

49 Hochschild (2016), p. 225; Durkheim (1965) [1915].

50 Reed (2001), p. 273.

51 Alexander (2016).

52 Covington (2012); Arendt (1958, 2003); Whitmer (2001).

53 Baldwin (1965) .

54 Anderson, C. (2017) "Derailing the Great Migration," pp. 39–66.

55 Douglass (1853).

56 See the account of colleague Jack Ringel in Chapter 2 for a discussion of his experience in a group which more or less descended into an emotional mob.

57 Sapolsky (2017), Chapter 11: "Us versus Them," pp. 387–424.

58 Wyatt-Brown (1991), an introductory essay on the life and work of W. J. Cash, pp. vii–xxxviii.

2

SEEKING SECURITY AMID EMOTIONAL TURBULENCE

We seek security in terms of maintaining inner and outer harmony. In our complex world the easiest path to harmony may be our reversion to simpler views of reality which involve seeming certainties. The price for this reversion is to forsake our capacities to recognize complex realities, which embrace uncertainty. This is a significant dilemma that individuals and nations face currently.

Reversion to "simpler realities"

Inner turbulence may be triggered by intense emotions and efforts to manage them. Modern neuroscience[1] gives us a way to understand the emergence of affective up-wellings as the source of energy for our coming alive. From this view, unless that upsurge is modified it may become internally overwhelming.

Our growth and development seem to go counter to the laws of physics which hold that all matter trends toward disorganization and decay. As thriving beings, we move in the direction of animation instead of de-animation. That is, we "swim upstream" against the sweep of entropic forces. Yet, at nearly every stage of growth and accomplishment there is uncertainty. Such disturbance may temporarily trigger reversion toward the seeming certainties from the earlier realm of action, impulse and absolutes. From the modern perspective of thought-based functioning, this more ancient mental world can be considered as a static tableau of polarized positions. That is, as a certainty that never changes. Since there is no space amidst this stasis for considered thought, there is no space for new ideas. Power, speed and certainty, the stuff of the jungle and perhaps the beginnings of authoritarian tribal rule, prevail.

We thus encounter different levels of reality based on the levels of development and the accrual of internal resources available. Generally speaking, access to the metabolizing functions of attentive care and its capacities to transform intense, even painful affect into potential thought and meaning are necessary for the upstream journey of mental and emotional development.

Early mechanisms distort reality in order to avoid disturbance. For example, *denial* leaves the impression that "nothing happened"; *projection*, likely based on the body's evacuative functions, expels the disturbance and attributes it to external sources. These externalizations likely utilize ancient herd-based modes of emotional transmission. *Dissociation* registers two conflicting views but keeps them separated by sectoring off alternate illusions of reality. These modes of protection involve some fragmentation of our capacities for whole-minded mental function. They distort the fullness of the reality that our integrated selves are capable of perceiving.

The mechanisms of *splitting and projection* may also halt this journey, as they are also efforts to rid oneself of unwanted aspects of experience. In expelling our negative experience, we not only split off our higher mental functions, but we likely slip into an endangered-seeming world, feeling now threatened by those who harbor the "bad" qualities that we have just disowned. Similarly, those targets are now felt out to rob or harm us, due to our feeling diminished by the very act of projecting away a part of ourselves. Actually, of course, when we utilize splitting and projection we do fracture and diminish our minds. We shear away not only our fears and uncertainties, but our spacious, thoughtful selves, which harbor the very capacities for the transformative thought that can offer rescue.

In our automatic attempt to find security by reverting to a simpler reality, then, we actually shear away stabilizing capacities for thought and self-regulation. Our effort to avoid the complex reality involving uncertainty leads us back into the pre-thinking, survival mentality of our ancestral selves. Without the spacious capacities of thought, we feel more subject to pressure, sensory intensity and impulsive action. The pressured experience is often phrased as "I have no time to slow down, to pay attention, to stop and think; I only feel pressured all the time." In my clinical experience, this pressure-based state regards spaciousness and quiet thought as weakness. From within this self-centered, sensory-defined state of mind, might makes right, and otherness is viewed as a potential threat. Our openness to others has not yet been developed in this simpler reality. Familiar tribal bonds reinforce the safety of a static certainty about friend and foe. Splitting and projection, then, foster reversion from open-hearted humanity to our more bunkered, tribal, pressured inhuman selves. We will explore this source of inhumanity in our consideration of group phenomena.

From another vantage point, consider whether the cerebral cortex, the physical residence of recently evolved mental capacities, beckons for mental integration.[2] Once there is splitting or cleavage, the pressures toward re-unification of the mind are feared as dangerous and destabilizing. The cleaved mind is then at war with itself: pressures toward re-unification are countered by pressures to re-enforce the conviction that all doubt, uncertainty and danger lie outside and must be kept at bay or in some way subdued. Otherwise, the fear contends, the disowned elements in the form of tormenting doubt (an internal tormentor) or the now-hated other (as external danger), may return violently to overwhelm the fractured mind. The feared repatriation of disowned aspects, then, in the absence of reflective thought and recognition, may become a re-union feared to lead to catastrophe.[3] Measured guidance by self-reflection and restraint, appreciative of the dangers of overwhelm, aid in the re-integrative processes.

The forces for unchanging stasis can entrap the mind for years, lifetimes, or generations in this sensory-based reality, where appearances and unquestioned traditions comprise "all there is." Any new idea is considered as betrayal or heresy. The myth of white supremacy in the American South, that should never be seen clearly for what it is, exemplifies this frozen state. Exposing the myth of the inferiority of the black man endangers unquestioned assumptions held as Truths. At times, it would seem to be a Herculean task to overcome such frozen dread of mental integration. To do so would be to expose the idealized white supremacist myth as a lie. And once that lie is revealed, the myth of grandeur and benevolence collapses, revealing the skeleton of brutality, greed and inhumanity. The culture of lynching and vicious vengefulness in the post-Reconstruction South might reveal this inhuman brutality as it attempted to justify Southern patriotism and the demonstration of white supremacy. Such violence-laced stasis may involve not only generations, but centuries of tribal feuding and frozen, hate-laced myths. It would take a whole new value system to welcome the over-turning of such myths and lies, one based more on care than fear.

Adhering to the group

Prior to the advent of individual thought, early man likely needed the protections of group mentality. Research suggests that modern-day humans still turn to group and tribal functioning to minimize disturbing emotions.[4] This reversion involves creating illusions and myths, of an idealized past where things were simple and uncertainty minimal. Such wished-for simplicity likely never really existed in modern life. But the longing for the seeming security of the strong tribe, possibly an echo from our evolutionary past, can heighten the allure for a charismatic leader whose strength and certainty, the myth continues, will lead the group to safety.[5] For many in the modern world who crave stability and value traditions, the group remains important, and can continue to supplant individual thoughts and opinions.[6]

Neurologists have observed that the social pressure to conform within a group does two things: it shuts down the prefrontal cortex where reasoning abides, while it also heightens the perceptual centers within the parietal and occipital regions of the brain. Our own thoughts, then, are not considered and we seem to perceive the predominant positions of others in the group.[7] The sense of belonging which groups offer stimulates the release of the hormone oxytocin, which re-enforces that well-being. In addition, this hormone also fosters defensive aggression toward non-group members. These powerful affects, which strengthen the bonds to the group, may outweigh any tendency to remain open to opposing thought, including science-based arguments.[8]

The sense of belonging to a group seems basic to primary identity. Whitmer[9] emphasizes how vital a receptive other mind is in establishing our sense of basic identity. He also suggests that we can easily dissociate or drift from knowing ourselves when we lack that needed affirmation. In addition, Haskell (2017) describes the Waorani tribe of the western Amazon region whose identity appears to be clearly defined by their relationship to their group. This report suggests that leaving the tribe is tantamount to withering exile at best, but more likely to suicide. Also, if one goes to another tribe the home tribe permanently erases that person's name, blocking any possibility of return.[10] This sense of betraying the group or betrayal by the group is closely linked with emotional or physical death, which harkens back to the suicide of historian W. Cash, following the publication of his book which exposed the myth of white supremacy and the largess of the Southern planter class.

Cognitive scientists also observe that the strong emotions of an intense experience imprint positive or negative thoughts and beliefs held as unassailable Truths. "Beliefs . . . (at) times of heightened emotion, especially . . . terror and dread, are . . . resistant to disconfirmation."[11] The history of white supremacy illustrates this observation with clarity. The psychological term "confirmation bias," is understood as a strong tendency to gloss over the shortcomings of ideas that mirror one's own, while vigorously attacking those that contradict one's views.[12] Strong emotion and confirmation bias are significant examples of the experience which can split the mind into intensely held positive and negative positions.

An example is offered by a colleague, Jack Ringel, LICSW,[13] who shared his experience during a professional gathering of fellow therapists. His account demonstrates how the contagion of powerful emotion can splinter and polarize the proceedings within a professional group discourse. For context, this convention was held during the politically turbulent time following the presidential inauguration of Donald Trump.

> Even among these professionals the group process mirrored the wider social/cultural tendency to descend from respectful discourse . . . What began as a soft rhythm quickly turned into a series of people literally standing and giving speeches . . . The tone was often accusatory of the "other" . . . while also claiming some order of self-righteousness. The splits between good and bad were proliferating. People began forming alliances, taking sides . . . I found it tremendously immobilizing and difficult to think (amidst the polarizing content and process) . . . many of the group's most seasoned attendees said that they'd never seen a large group quite like this among colleagues . . . One went as far as to say, during the group itself, "this isn't a large group at all!" . . . implying that a group requires connection (rather than alienating harangue) to be called such.

Jack offered reflections about the experience, including his emotional responses:

> Sitting in the large group felt like being a part of a loosely integrated organism; I was me (with my own mind) when I walked in, but that mind felt increasingly bombarded by strong currents of emotion, sometimes so strong and confusing that I couldn't make sense of them. One of my only comments . . . was on the third day when I said, "I feel so much sadness. This feels like a funeral to me". That association fit with a dream shared by another participant earlier in the day, which

involved the burying of . . . coffins . . . There were small glimpses of hope – moments when speech-giving gave way to vulnerability and (emotional) connection (with self and other) – but they were no more than that: glimpses. Interestingly, once the group ended, I found an older gentleman whom I knew and with tears in our eyes we both hugged and felt very close. I found other friends and even strangers, and similarly, we shared both physical affection (handshakes, hugs) and words imbued with love and empathy . . . And yet, while the group was still happening, it felt like we were on separate islands, shouting to one another, the words often lost in the chop of the surf.

Jack notes, further, the similarity between this group's dynamics and those on the larger canvass of national politics:

the dynamics seemed to mirror – in a remarkably close way – what was happening on a larger cultural, social, and political level with regard to presidential and other politics. People were giving speeches, but not listening to each other . . . the large group never did seem to cohere and heal. Scapegoating was abundant, as was a general tone of anger and tribalism.

And perhaps as a postscript, Jack offers further reflection:

(how) my initial recounting of (the group experience) described the process, at least in part, as something that I wasn't fully a part of . . . Most strikingly, I didn't initially speak about how I, too, was very much caught up in the splitting and projection ("the torches were being lit" [a reference to a group dissolving into a mob] applied to me at times, too, even if it was almost entirely an internal process for me, aside from some non-verbal communication). Feeling a part of the group, but also not part of it . . . It seems to be another iteration of "us and them" thinking, and perhaps the . . . (primitive emotional) contagion making its way through the room that day.

I agreed with my colleague that his experience of only being partially present, and having difficulty mentioning that in his account suggested the experience when one's mind succumbs to the splitting processes. Here the personality is cleaved so that there is less of a sense of a coherent presence in one's own experience or when trying to recall the encumbering events.

Powerful, destabilizing emotions can be heightened when the group leader has charismatic qualities, someone who has a personality compelling to members of the group. These qualities often go against convention and offer promise of new possibilities to those who have felt besieged or overlooked.[14] This charismatic individual, emboldened by a sense of power, feels himself to be the longed-for savior. When his un-opposable position is challenged, his conviction of threat is intensified and he pressures his group into views of the challenge as a dangerous, opposing enemy.[15] Historian Ayers, cited in the previous chapter, noted that the neighboring Northern and Southern towns became harsher and more polarized in their views as the Civil War neared. Examples of this same tendency can be seen in current political situations where opposing opinions harden positions. Then groups can seem increasingly warlike when any opposition to their chosen candidate is expressed. These issues will be examined further in Chapter 4 detailing tyranny and the confrontation of tyrannical leaders.

A dangerous situation may develop if the charismatic leader whips his/her group up into violence against the opposition. Understanding his/her internal dynamics may be of help in terms of maintaining a thinking mind. Intensely held views that characterize the charismatic leader can easily become convictions. That is, these views become un-opposable Truths. Opposing conviction feels like a catastrophe to the one holding it, because in part he/she has no way to think about the parts of reality that run counter to the certainty of the conviction. Any confrontation compels him/her to project rigidity to the outside, thus "creating" a heroic-seeming war between the assumedly powerful attacking other and the perceived-to-be weakened heroic self.[16] Clinical experience suggests that the intensity of the conviction is directly proportional to the degree of threat perceived. This view may lead one to the conclusion that the power of conviction rests in part on the degree of threat the conviction perceives to its absolutism. If the threat feels intense, the absolutism will be re-affirmed. There is no questioning, just powerful adherence to the conviction as a bastion which requires defense. An adherent to the conviction, then, in being overturned becomes a martyr in the eyes of those holding the conviction. These findings will be interesting to hold in mind when we turn attention to aspects of tyranny in Chapter 4.[17]

When the charismatic leader has mesmerized his followers into believing that he alone can be their savior, they abandon doubts about the quality of his leadership.[18] The intensity of the leader's comments, then, become Truths to his followers. Excitement is felt to be nourishment, even to opposing states of mind. Clarity of thought may well be obscured, because such minds may also become excited in terms of outrage, and thus lose thinking capacities needed to critically evaluate the charismatic leader's declarations.

Normal mental and emotional development organizes experience by categorizing and separating positive from negative experience or expectation. A subsequent stage fosters the recognition that negative and positive views can be held toward the same important figure, such as a parent, loved by the dependent part of the personality while also hated by the part that wishes to get its way with no frustration. The capacity to hold both views in a relatively balanced way is often termed as ambivalence. Such balance can be lost when polarizing pressures, such as frustration or peer pressure, are present. In groups where each member is subject to operating according to the trends within the group, polarized views tend to predominate. The group is likely to become galvanized into a single conviction, or view of reality. In this circumstance, neutral facts or any view that differs from the group view can be easily dismissed or attacked. In the current political climate, unfavored facts can be dismissed as "Fake News". Once again, "If a study supports our ideas we tend to gloss over shortcomings, but if it contradicts them we attack with ruthless vigor, picking apart every detail possible."[19] Group loyalty becomes paramount and it takes a great deal of dissonance to alter the group's view of its position.

The recent history of gun control in the United States may illustrate this situation. The wording of the Second Amendment of the U.S. Constitution, stipulating the right to bear arms, is not specific as to whether the right is a collective or an individual one. For many years in the United States, up until the 1970s, the tendency had been to consider it a collective one. In fact, after the assassinations of John Kennedy, Martin Luther King, and the attempt on Ronald Reagan which left his aide Jim Brady gravely wounded, the tendency to become more restrictive of guns seemed to be the trend in much of the nation. However, apparently with suspicion of the government growing due to the Watergate scandal and to the outcome of the Vietnam War, a right-wing group of the National Rifle Association (NRA) at its national convention in 1978 managed to insert into leadership members who emphasized the interpretation of the Second Amendment as by far favoring the individual right to bear arms.[20] Strong advocates from this section of the NRA have continued to erroneously stress that the Second Amendment is exclusively about the individual's right to bear arms, overlooking the long tradition in the country of the collective right. In addition, they have continued to urge the acquisition of firearms both to assuage citizens' fears and to extol manliness.[21]

These factors and increasing populism in the United States have pre-vented the successful passage of effective gun control legislation, even with the significant increase in mass shootings in recent years. The pro-gun lobby has responded to these mass shooting events by amassing more firearms for protection, that is, following the recommendations of the NRA. From the position of the pro-gun lobby, this is the Second Amendment at work; but the gun control lobby might view this position, in the face of these shooting events, as a continuing conviction based less on thought and more on reac-tivity to unwarranted fear, the equation of guns to manliness, and to group adherence.

Notes

1 Solms (2013).
2 Fuster (2001); Preston (2013); Nee, Jahn, & Brown (2014).
3 I have addressed the experience of this dread of reunification in a previous pub-lication (Anderson, M., 2016) but as I feel that it is at the heart of the message of the book, I will excerpt it here and again in Chapter 7:

> Reintegration involves the repatriation of . . . (externalized) disturbance as part of self. This process means realizing that not only the obstructing dis-turbances, but also the divisive forces that aim to disown the disturbances, are not external. Such recognition indeed annihilates the myth of being the power at the centre of the world and re-establishes the humbler proces-sive to and fro involved in learning. In lived experience this clear view and dismantling of . . . (the hard shell of certainty) is not a gentle process. It is one that involves bearing pain and tension as one softens the hardened cara-pace, risking feeling humiliated, as one owns the disavowed elements, before feeling the relief of reunion. In the lived moment, that pain and tension involve the risk of embracing need, which has been felt as weakness, trust taking the place of cynicism, attentive care seen as other than manipulation or domination. As mentioned, this reunification process may involve a jarring and then dis-arming shift from power to the wider awareness of vulnerability and need, as humiliation trends toward humility. (pp. 91–92)

4 Gorman & Gorman (2017); Sapolsky (2017), pp. 387–424; pp. 425–477; Nicholson (1998).
5 This tendency to harken back nostalgically to a fantasied golden era is discussed by Timothy Snyder (2017) in his compelling discussion about tyranny, which will be discussed in some detail in the next chapter. It is interesting to consider the evolutionary and psychological roots of this nostalgic allure.
6 In traditional Eastern cultures the group still predominates, the role of the individual being less emphasized. So, the perspectives here refer primarily to Western cultures, where individuality is more emphasized. McGilchrist (2009), pp. 452–459.
7 Gorman & Gorman (2017), p. 96.

8 *Ibid.*, p. 99 This book offers an informing discussion of factors which support denial of science: preference for simplicity, complex thought requiring work; the power of affect to sway opinion; positions which involve strong emotion burning deeper into the mind as 'truths' than more softly held rational or scientific views; the power of the group, which includes feeling we belong or share the group's opinions as far more pleasurable than pesky science-based reasoning. The works of several authors are cited. A psychoanalytic reader, here, finds verification for the power of splitting and projection, and the need for integrative thought as rescue from this hard-edged denialism.

9 Whitmer (2001).

10 Haskell (2017), pp. 3–30.

11 Gorman & Gorman (2017), p. 131; Hertz, 2013, p. 38.

12 Gorman & Gorman (2017), pp. 107, 108, 137.

13 I am very grateful to Jack for his detailed offering which allows the reader to nearly be present in that experience.

14 Attempts to assess the sentiment of the electorate in mid-2017 reveal the power of group adhesion and polarization in contemporary American politics as reflected in the following references: Theodoridis (2015); Huddy, Mason, & Aaroe (2015); Iyengar, Sood, & Lelkes (2012).

15 Gorman & Gorman (2017), pp. 79–81.

16 This scenario of heroic efforts against a monstrous enemy is amply portrayed in the language of Joseph McCarthy, cited in Chapter 4.

17 Gorman & Gorman (2017), pp. 79–81.

18 Students of Wilfred Bion will recognize his description of the basic group fantasy of an all-powerful rescuing figure in this clinical description. Part of the allure of this promise that 'only I can fix it' can be attributed to this basic longing.

19 Gorman & Gorman (2017), pp. 107, 108, 137.

20 Lopez (2018).

21 Sedaris (2018).

PART II

The mind faces feared realities: Rescue via courage and attentive care

The most primary quest for safety and security shapes the mind's functioning. Hard-wired to expect basic care, which I note as CARE, in its presence the personality thrives. But the trauma and pain experienced in the absence of CARE introduces or revivifies regressive modes of functioning which involve the fragmentation of the mind. Part of the potential tragedy, here, is that this mental splintering actually introduces violence which triggers the mental world of seeming enemies. The resulting fear-based polarization freezes the potential to get to know that "enemy" as the expelled debris of one's own shattered mind. A warzone mentality can develop which may entrap the individual and the group in hostile standoffs as sworn enemies.

Such frozen polarizations can tragically preclude the greatest potential for rescue, the CARE-bringing mind capable of bearing divisive fears and terrors. This wider-ranging mind can also realize that various realities may pertain at the same time. It can bear to empathically suffer the pain of accountability, vital for the transformation of the polarized view into one of many potential views. This rescuing state of mind, then, ferries the journey between the realities based on power and those based on humanity.[1]

This section of the book, then, turns to this rescuing potential. In Chapter 3 we examine the basic elements of CARE and the consequences of its absence. We then examine the external manifestations of the retreat from CARE and whole-mindedness. In Chapter 4 we consider confrontations with tyranny, which threaten to arise when authoritarianism offers the false promise of restoration and security to a fearful, fragmented people. The needed confrontation, involving more integrated minds and the quiet retention of personal authority, can view the hollowness and danger of the authoritarian threat. Chapter 5 deals with the inner realizations needed for trust and faith to maintain personal integration through potential hard times. The exploration highlights some of the underpinnings of steadfast hope and courage. The contrast between an ethic based on power, and an ethic based on courage and faith will be offered. Chapter 6 will carry this theme of internal integration forward, with European as well as further American views. Chapter 7 offers summary reflections of the major themes of the book.

3

SEEKING SECURITY VIA CARE AND THOUGHT

Our infantile selves seek security via maternal care. We seem to have a nascent anticipation that a care-bringing presence will tend to our earliest disturbance, making it better.[2] Wilfred Bion postulated that a variety of innate anticipations or "preconceptions," shape the psyche in terms of being "realized" or experienced in post-natal life.[3] Further, close observation of earliest mother-infant interplay[4] strongly suggests that mammalian evolution has hard-wired the expectation for a care-bringing presence. I refer to the object of this innate expectation, then, as well as the internalization of this capacity, as CARE.

Modern views of psychic development[5] suggest that each of us learns to bear the swirl of unmediated reality via the presence of an attentive other, someone who soothes the tensions and distresses from internal (hunger, pain, fear) as well as external (sudden or startling sensory experience) sources. This attentive presence, be it the mother, the household, or the village, offers a buffering, metabolizing function. Part of this CARE involves focused attention that labels, and thus transforms, distressing experience into meaning ("you're feeling hungry . . . you were startled by that loud noise"). This intermediary mothering function between the earliest nascent self and the presentations of the world, often referred to as reverie, helps the emerging self to make sense of the world and its own experience. In addition, it is a primary source not only of our well-being but also of our humanity. Reverie, deriving from maternal love, demonstrates patience and compassion in receiving and translating external distresses and internal eruptions and rages without retaliation. The temporal space that is part of the experience of patience is also a template for the establishment of the inner space needed for reflective thought.[6] Reverie and its gifts, then, may be equated with what we generally term as maternal love, and open-heartedness.[7] It is also the template for inclusiveness, and openness to change, growth and the new idea.

Bearing emotional storms, of course, can be wearing for even the most devoted mothering persons. Indeed, each of us learns to harbor a certain quality of this compassionate CARE according to how we ourselves were cared for. Certainly, inborn temperament is very important in terms of the baby's neural and psychic equipment. However, the pairing of maternal and infant rhythms which occurs throughout pregnancy likely sets the stage for the ongoing interplay as the parent-infant pair confronts the growing complexity of the outer and the inner worlds they encounter in earliest post-natal life and beyond. External CARE, then, becomes the template for internal CARE, to which the cerebral cortex is nearly entirely dedicated.[8]

Neuroscientific perspectives of CARE

Looking at the need for CARE from more detailed neuroscience perspectives reveals that these cerebral functions, shaped initially by care-giving others, mediate the arousals from deep within the brainstem, the most primitive part of the brain thought to occur in all vertebrates.[9] These primary centers of activation seem to arouse the quiescent organism in its efforts to come alive. These internal up-wellings or affects[10] need to be recognized and modulated by the most recently evolved portions of the brain, the cerebral cortex, for the human individual to become organized and regulated in adaptive, growth-promoting patterns. Otherwise, a chaotic flooding from internal sources (as might be seen in inconsolability or uncontainable tantrums) may become the matrix for the personality.

Splitting mechanisms predominate amidst the early defenses. Splitting is defined here as the cleavage of the mind such that the capacities for reflection and self-regulation are shorn away. This separation from cortical functioning leaves the more ancient survival modes to be experienced concretely as "how it is" rather than "how I feel and think about my experience." Splitting, then, re-introduces the experience of being plunged into the potential flood of unmediated affects and anxieties, unprotected by the reverie function, which would bring thought and meaning.

Splitting may also be thought of creatively, as the invocation of a level of neural functioning which sharply separates intensely felt negative input from softer, more positive experience. It also helps to organize experience into "bad" and "good" and to shape protective responses, such as denial ('it didn't happen') or projection ("he/she is the source of my pain"). As the personality matures, with proper external and internal care and containment, it can bear more exposure to the complexity of reality, including more conscious recognition and responsibility for its own emotions. In these circumstances, or with CARE, the earliest modes of managing distress (denial, splitting and projection) will generally give way to more adaptive coping, such as identification with CARE-giving figures and self-regulating thought.

This sense of care and well-being has been discovered to be registered by the body in terms of a robust immune system. Several epigenetic studies, register how immediate experience, both positive and negative, can alter gene function, verifying the impact of CARE on overall functioning and well-being.[11] In the absence of such restraining CARE, however, these early forms of defense may become more generalized as personality traits, limiting opportunities to adapt to reality that more mature coping skills would foster. Other observations[12] demonstrate the value of even the occasional experience of a reliable presence to the well-being of vulnerable individuals. Humanizing containment, which includes reflective thought and physical well-being, appears to be among our most evolved capacities. But, interestingly, modern cultural attitudes vary with regards to what constitutes this aspect of care.

Conservative Americans, who favor small government and individual initiative, often consider governmental programs for children's welfare as intrusion into parental choice and perhaps coddling the child. Liberals view these programs as offering an enriching environment for everyone, but perhaps especially to families who otherwise might be struggling. Nordic countries, on the other hand, having the opportunity to rebuild social structures following the devastations of World War II, have adopted the philosophy of providing an enriching environment for all citizens. This relieves the parents and frees the children from the anxiety of where provisions will come from. Such environmental provision is geared to foster personal freedom and autonomy, encouraging each individual to determine his/her own autonomy without dependence upon parents, spouses or employers for financial services such as health care, education, and aid in crises.[13]

Another relevant issue here is the registration of negative, painful experience: we remember our painful experiences, including our losses, more intensely than we do positive experiences.[14] This may seem puzzling, but it is likely due to lessons from evolution: painful experience, readily recallable, may trigger protective avoidance whereas the recall of positive experience may seem an unnecessary luxury.

Differences between the development and functions of the right and the left cerebral hemispheres provides further understanding. Both hemispheres work in a coordinated way for the fullness of function, but there are specific differences in function which are interesting to consider.[15] The right hemisphere matures significantly earlier than the left and seems to be fairly fully functioning at birth. With its intense focus on bodily, visual and spatial sensory modes, it seems to pay attention to our somatic well-being, including our intuitive "gut" feelings. It also fosters visual and spatial orientation in both the inner and the outer world. In short, right-hemispheric function seems to register and to present aspects of our pre-verbal and non-verbal experience in bodily, somatic ways. Its early maturation likely also aids the registration of implicit (unremembered) experience. Due to the right brain's wide-ranging, sensory-based sources, it appears to be the greatest source for our intuition, while its functions remain mostly out of awareness. In order for aspects of experience to come into conscious awareness, the capacity for self-reflection and language is generally necessary.[16]

This is where the vital importance of left hemispheric functions come into play. These include language, fine motor development and minutely focused attention, functions which seem to have developed to aid the emergence of consciousness and the growth of civilizations and, indeed, human domination of the earth and its resources. It has been observed by those who have suffered impairment of these regions,[17] that these left hemispheric functions develop an attitude of "knowing everything" and of expressing contempt toward the more silent but wide-ranging perspectives of the right brain. These more dominating functions, based mostly on language, detailed categorization, and abstraction focus attention, thus present us with compelling language-based "truths." The satisfaction that accompanies such certainties likely contributes to the emotionally omnipotent triumph that language-based convictions can arouse. From our present view, these left hemispheric functions likely play a powerful role in maintaining myths, based on unquestioned convictions, such as those of white supremacy. Such myths preclude the wider realizations of reality that the right-hemispheric functions would allow. A final integrative step would require the "knowings" of the left hemisphere to be surrendered back to the right-hemispheric intuitions, such as "sleeping on it before sending that email." This may be difficult to do when left hemispheric certainty feels compelling.

Another more recently studied cerebral function may also be considered to be an internal source of attentive CARE. Certain parts of the cerebral cortex in both hemispheres light up in fMRI studies when the individual is not paying focused attention on certain tasks, including active thought. The term "default mode network"[18] (DMN) has been ascribed to these areas, which, at first glance, might seem to be the brain at rest. However, this state of apparent quietude seems to involve a network where integrative work occurs, such as anticipation of the future from memories of previous experience. Such integration may also involve the stitching together of a narrative of self and others. The basic personality is perhaps shaped by the DMN, which may contribute significantly to the cortical source of attentive CARE and the transformation of sensory intensity into meaning. When the DMN is functioning minimally, we may become lost or trapped in the flood of our emotions. Alternatively, when the DMN and other cortical functions are activated, we may better observe rather than be caught in the flood of emotion. Such is the mediation and stability offered by the integrating functions of the cerebral cortex, the overall residence of considered thought as well as CARE.

When CARE is not forthcoming

When that expectation of CARE is *not* met, the self, feeling overwhelmed from unmediated internal or external stimuli, may experience destabilizing surprise in the form of a disappointment so jarring as to seem catastrophic. The absence of anticipated CARE, then, in the failure to provide the template for the modulating cortical capacities, may trigger the experience of despair, dread, or the sense of being only worthy of abandonment and abuse.[19] Careful observers note that children who have been neglected or abused themselves are quite likely to neglect or abuse others, as if "this is how it is' . . . this is how my family relates; anything else is not part of the world that I know." Psychologists speak of identification with the aggressor, insecure attachment patterns, psychopathic, or deeply narcissistic personalities, according to the perspective of the observer. Unrealized CARE leaves the nascent self feeling helpless and alone. The spectrum of negating experience from abandonment and neglect may trigger intrusive, sadistic, and even life-threatening behavior.[20] The background sense of the world as a benign or a malevolent place may, then, be strongly shaped by these early templates of the presence or absence of CARE.

While the individual may be raised attentively, the background of unquestioned assumptions of 'how things are' easily becomes internalized as part of "who we are . . . who I am." For example, a child born into a culture which embraces the myth of white supremacy may silently absorb that assumption as part of his/her group identity, relating to the myth as a given, as "how it is." So, the myth may continue as an unquestionable assumption, deflecting any curiosity that a sensitive, growing mind might apply. But for some within that culture there is a deeply disturbing consideration that the myth is really a lie. How the individual deals with this almost unbearable conflict is an important question. The Southern author, W. J. Cash, apparently could not bear his own exposure of the myth as a lie; it very likely drove him to suicide. It is possible that most people could not bear to be fully aware that such a deeply embedded myth is a lie; they would have to employ denial, dissociation or splitting and projection. The use of these mental mechanisms would likely disempower the capacity for clear-minded thought.

The impoverished personality as a consequence of CARE *un*met

When the child feels well cared for his inner urges are likely channeled creatively, such as in an accruing curiosity about himself and the world. Where attentive CARE has not been experienced, that is, where the CARE-bringing environment for whatever reason is unavailable, the child may feel neglected. In these situations, curiosity about oneself and the world may, in turn, be severely curtailed. Indeed, the child may be feeling apathetic and unworthy of care, and thus may then encounter a sense of despair about ever being able to vitalize itself. The sense of hollowness, ennui, or "being nothing of interest" might prevail.

Further, the child in this situation, not having felt held in mind via the focused attention of others, cannot begin to differentiate aspects of its own experience. That is, this child may not be able to distinguish between input from the external world or from its own affective perceptions. Along with internal apathy, there may also be verbal or motoric outbursts as attempts to rid oneself of distress or accumulating tension. As well, one caught in a swirl of emotion may feel at one with that swirl, and thus part of the chaotic flow as "who I am and what the world is about." A defensive response to such chaos may be complete overwhelm, or a state of mind that some psychoanalysts have termed as omnipotence because of the massive identification of the self as being bigger than life, and without human limits or boundaries. This state appears to carry with it the illusion or perhaps delusion of complete self-sufficiency, needing nothing, owning the world.

While the outside viewer may then see desperate expressions of self-sufficiency or bravado, the inner experience, without a helping other, is one of desperate efforts to survive or to succumb to the pressure of the chaos. This disconnect between inner experience and outer view is thought to be bridged by sturdy CARE. Only when there has been an experience of a helping, soothing, containing other does CARE provide the necessary differentiation of self, other, and the world.

Attentive CARE introduces the relatively undifferentiated psyche to the world in gradual doses; tensions are made bearable via rhythmic soothing, and distresses are calmed by attentive ministrations to bodily and emotional needs. Gradual exposure to reality allows differentiation, accommodation and maturation. But the child, caught in the less differentiated omnipotent state of mind, experiences a different reality. Amidst the internal swirl chaos defines reality; indeed, that chaos may be relabeled as "freedom" and efforts to bind or modulate the outpouring seen as "curtailing my power." Potentially containing boundaries, such as firm holding during an escalating tantrum, then would likely be experienced as impediments. This child, caught in the swirl of unbridled emotion, hates the adult's efforts of restraint, while also desperately needing that containment in order to find rescue from the uncontained emotion. The helpless outrage triggered in this experience for both parent and child can be very painful to bear.[21] This child, being observed by a calmer other mind, may feel that mind not as a soothing presence but more as brutal or humiliating impingement or scrutiny. The presence of that separate mind may challenge the omnipotent assumption that one's inner intensity is the only reality. The child's tantrum and hatred of the calm, containing parent is a painful, but vivid example of this situation.

This conflict with difference also impairs learning because the function of learning challenges the omnipotent stance of knowing everything. Here, then, boundaries which might protect and contain are felt as entrapping constraints. Most painfully, for the omnipotently oriented, yet undifferentiated self, doubt is equated with foolishness or stupidity. The normally developing child gradually learns that doubt accompanies all new explorations. But the state of mind which cannot bear to learn may experience doubt as a terror. The superior attitude of knowing everything may be considered as an attempt to keep at bay the underlying fear, loneliness, and dread which mark this less differentiated state of mind that either refused or was somehow bypassed by the ministrations of attentive CARE.

The individual bereft of CARE is then caught amidst arousing and exciting stimuli, which might have little lasting value. Where sensory excitement prevails, there can be little or no sense of transforming that excitement into meaningful thought. Indeed, in severe circumstances of neglect there may be little actual thought occurring and, perhaps, no concept of space for thought. Instead, the individual may feel filled with exciting stimuli as "evidence" of being the most active, aggressive, glittering, individual around. A blustery presentation often bolsters a very fragile interior.

Such individuals attempt to gain protection via the primary defenses of denial ("there is no danger") and projection ("it's all his fault"). Without the self-modulation that CARE can bestow, doubt and negativity must be externalized as blame. Amidst ever-hovering inundation one cannot envision benign growth. The known and the unchanging promise immediate protection and safety, while the unknown triggers a sense of dread.

A further element here is the attitude and fantasy toward thought that others engage in, but which the unmodulated self cannot embrace. Thought that one cannot engage in is often felt as that held by an "elite other" who "thinks him- or herself to be so much better than me." This distortion is a useful, if painful, example of the distortions which splitting and projection lead to; that is, a splitting of experience into bad and good. Such may be the situation among the working-class Americans concerned about the day to day continuity of work and place and family, who view the college or coastal elites with the liberal agenda as looking down on them. But, those so-called elites, privileging change and inclusion, are often out of touch with the values of loyalty, place, and the traditions of the white working class. Indeed, the vulnerable self, feeling seen by another, almost reflexively feels scrutinized and looked down upon. It takes a good deal of self-confidence, based on comfort with oneself and one's impulses, usually acquired by access to sturdy CARE, to foster the shift from this feeling of scrutiny to the sense of being observed from a benign perspective.

The individual, then, who cannot feel nourished by thought operates on the level of sensory-based excitement, arousal, and power. The recent "Post-Truth Era" can be understood as an era in which quiet thought, based on facts and borne in respect, is not the coin of the realm in terms of communication and value. Instead, what appeals are the emotions that can be stirred, the projection of accountability as "his fault," and the momentary "tweet" which can expel one's temporary thought, to then be dismissed. There is little if any capacity for considered, nourishing thought in this state of mind.

Notes

1 The thoughtful reader may in considering this mental fragmentation be reminded of civil wars in external as well as internal reality but also about current polarizations which seem to be so endangering for the whole-minded functioning of the American polity. These musings are among those which prompted the writing of this book.

2 Trevarthan (1996).

3 Bion (1962).

4 Earliest mother–infant interplay: Mancia (1981); Trevarthan (1996); Friston (2010).

5 Modern views of psychic development: Bion (1962); Civitarese (2011).

6 It seems that the neural correlates for orientation to external and internal space are located in the right associational cortex. Kaplan-Solms and Solms (2000), p. 198.

7 Anderson, M. (2016), chapters 6 and 7, pp. 97–111.

8 Kaplan-Solms & Solms (2000), Chapter 10, pp. 243–284.

9 Thought to occur in all vertebrates: Panksepp (1998).

10 Up-wellings often considered as affects: Solms (2013); Panksepp (2013).

11 Overall functioning and well-being: Kaufman et al. (2004); Anderson, M. (2016); Sapolsky (2017), p. 222.

12 Kaufman et al. (2004); Brooks (2016).

13 Partanen (2017).

14 Kanouse & Hanson (1972); Baumeister, Finkenauer, & Vohs (2001).

15 Differences in function which are interesting to consider: McGilchrist (2009) gives an especially rich and detailed account of the differences between the functions of the right and the left cerebral hemispheres. It serves as a major resource for this book, as will be noted in subsequent chapters.

Also, in a previous publication (Anderson, M. 2016) offers some integrative understanding of both cognitive and intuitive functions as they serve integration.

16 Solms (2003).

17 Bolte Taylor (2008a, 2008b).

18 "*default mode network*": Buckner et al. (2008); Spunt et al. (2015).

19 Gurevich (2008); Ferenczi (1988), pp. 8–10, 16–19.

20 Maiello (2000).

21 The turbulence experienced by both parent and child can be extra-ordinary, and often the parent cannot remain patient and steadfast, but himself/herself feels penetrated by the aggression, thus becoming at least somewhat reactive and possibly retaliatory. This not uncommon aspect of being a parent with human limits may illustrate also the limits of transformative care in and for all of us.

4

LESSONS DERIVED FROM CARE, COURAGE AND SELF-RESPECT

Timothy Snyder, a Professor of Modern European history at Yale University, has written on the forces of tyranny which have bedeviled Europe in recent times. In his recent book, *On Tyranny: Twenty Lessons from the Twentieth Century*, tyranny is described as "the usurpation of power . . . by rulers for their own benefit."[1] He notes how the Founding Fathers feared that the American democracy would be vulnerable to such take over. In this pithy book, Snyder suggests that Americans are currently as vulnerable to falling under tyrannical rule as those who fell under fascism in the last century. He suggests that we have the advantage of possibly learning from their experience, offering several such lessons. He brings to our attention the tendency to obey others who seem to be in charge.

Part of the legacy of World War II involved investigating man's capacity for inhumanity, such as how ordinary people could become part of the death squads which served the Nazi masters. In the early 1960s Stanley Milgram, a psychology professor at Yale University, set up experiments regarding blind obedience to authority. He was astonished to discover how well-meaning Americans could give up their own authority to the authoritative other (a man in a white coat in this experiment) even when that other was ordering torture to be meted out to unseen individuals.[2] The subjects of the experiment were directed to give what they felt were electric shocks to aid the "learning" of another person in the next room. Unknown to the subject the "learner" was faking the pain experienced as the subject obeyed the commands of the authority to increase the intensity of the shocks. Milgram demonstrated that even when the experimental subjects felt they were causing great pain, a majority of them carried out the authority's command. The documenting films[3] are agonizing to watch, as the viewer witnesses the torment of the subject caught in the conflict between inflicting harm and the seeming dictate of the experimenter. Possibly, part of the pain for the observer of the film involves witnessing the fragmentation of the subject's personality, the bypassing of the subject's own moral dictate, as he submits to the authoritarian other.

There has been much controversy about this experiment's findings. Some have wondered whether Milgram manipulated some of the data to make blind obedience even more striking than predicted. But to see even one of the subjects caught in such a dilemma aids our appreciation of the effects of the submission to the authority of a powerful other. Psycho-analytically, we might speculate that the harshness of one's internal self-critic might be a significant factor in terms of one's allegiance to external authority. But it is disturbing, even when one feels torn by authoritarian dictates. Even so, it is disturbing to see how one can easily slip from humanity into seemingly inhuman behavior.

Another psychology experiment, done in the early 1970s, demonstrated even more convincingly how healthy individuals can slip from compassion into dehumanizing roles. This experiment offered a further example of the splitting processes: individuals quickly became defined by their uniforms as either a sadistic guard or a helpless prisoner. The Stanford Prison Experiment[4] was conducted in 1971 by Phil Zimbardo, a professor of psychology at Stanford University, who undertook this study to consider the impact of imprisoning institutions on everyday individuals. He enlisted twenty-four healthy male students who were randomly assigned to be guards or prisoners, in an experiment advertised to be about personalities exposed to prison environments. The basement of the psychology building of Stanford University was turned into a mock prison. The randomly assigned "prisoners," delivered to the prison after being "arrested" and transported by the Palo Alto Police Department, were initially stripped, deloused and given shapeless prison gowns to wear, dress which served to erase their individuality. The "guards" wore khaki uniforms, reflecting sunglasses and Billy clubs, gear to enhance their inhumanity.[5] The experiment was set to run for two weeks. Surprisingly, each participant rapidly fell into role. Initially advised that they could leave the experiment at any time, slipping into role appeared to obscure this escape hatch for the participants. Zimbardo, along with being the chief investigator of the experiment, had also assigned himself to be the superintendent of the prison. For Zimbardo this role included his becoming protective of his "interesting experiment," so that he could not view the wider reality that healthy students were breaking down under the strain of the imprisoning environment. Feeling truly imprisoned, the student/prisoners were often overcome by helpless rage, resulting in serious mental decompensation for some. Also, one guard appeared to be steeped in escalating sadism, perhaps prompted by the lack of restraint as well as provocations from the prisoners. The lack of a compassionate overseer of this whole enterprise, a function we are calling CARE in this book, probably contributed to the escalating dyscontrol.

This experiment could not be replicated today due to ethical constraints. However, the experiment underlines how rapidly one can fall into role, losing touch with his or her personal freedom and choice when imprisoned within an entrapping myth. An experiment becomes a prison with no escape. Zimbardo could not realize his own imprisonment as the superintendent involved with his "interesting experiment" until a valued colleague brought to his attention that these were healthy young men who were being subjugated to tormenting conditions. Only when the whistle was blown could the spell be broken. That sudden realization did lead to the experiment being halted on day six rather than after two weeks.

A further lesson is that one cannot really stand astride two realities simultaneously, as Professor Zimbardo attempted to do. When absorbed in an experience one cannot also observe it. The more softly held experience of viewing the wider reality gives way to the more intense river of emotional experience. Put differently, the reality of personal choice and freedom of thought seems to be easily overturned by slipping into a role or a myth that defines who is in power and what can be thought or done. This is another significant lesson in terms of protecting one's personal authority via self-respect and CARE.[6]

From our retrospective view, it would be easy to criticize these experimenters and their seemingly inhuman experiments. A more compassionate view would realize these dedicated psychologists were earnestly trying to investigate the seemingly inhuman behavior which led to atrocities during World War II. Furthermore, academic psychology had not yet fully realized the need for ethical guidelines. We, in the decades since, have learned a lot but have much more to learn about our fragile humanity and how easily we can dip into our inhumanity.

Snyder's *Twenty Lessons* remind us to believe in the truth and to be on the alert for perversions of the truth, such as "fake news" and "alternative facts." We have seen some underpinnings for these distortions in the view of the group which eschews all contradictory facts or premises. Snyder also cautions us about the tendency to consider privacy violations as newsworthy. We all have impulses to get in on the inside of gossip, or to feel we are being kept out of important news, rather than to realize that in our wish for 'the scoop' we might actually be betraying the privacy of others. Appreciating boundaries also protects our own thinking, as such helps us to resist descent into the excitement of 'what are they saying and thinking' as breaking news. The allure of hidden so-called truths must be resisted.

Snyder also urges active confrontation of tyrannical motives. A courageous voice may be necessary to break the spell, as seen in the whistle blower in the Stanford Prison Experiment. Other examples include Rosa Parks' refusing to sit in the back of the bus, and of course Churchill standing up to the Nazis. Standing up means retaining the courage of one's authentic separate view as demonstrated by the counter-protests against the white nationalist march in Charlottesville, and the 30,000-strong counter-protest in Boston a week later.

The tyrant and his quest for power may be closely linked to paranoia. And paranoia, uncontained, may lead to chaos. Basically, paranoia involves a mind fractured by fear or other disturbing emotions, such that it cannot bear to own its fragments, pain or unsavory elements. For the budding tyrant the fantasy of omnipotence and manipulations toward power may defend against unrecognized insecurities. In any case, unwanted parts of the self may be violently projected onto or often into an external target, as a way of attempting to rid oneself of the disturbance. One consequence of such projection, however, is that the personality is not only further fragmented but it is also impoverished, part of itself having been ejected in the projection. Another consequence is that now that unwanted part of the self is felt to be an external threat, which in turn must be controlled or gotten rid of, as well. The violence emanating from the intense projections of parts of the self can in turn cause chaos because the force of those projections may destabilize all thinking minds nearby and leave instead a morass of fear, doubt and despair. The rescue from this situation, the attentive CARE needed, requires a sturdy mind which is able to stand up to and to confront the paranoia or tyrannical elements and label its destructive impact rather than to be defined and shattered by its accusations. This containment is necessary in order to break the spell of the "fixed idea" of those accusations, which would demand to be considered as indisputable truths. This confrontation and containment are needed as well in order to restore the capacities for calm, generative thought to those who have received and been beleaguered by the projections. It is also likely that the paranoid (here, tyrannical) individual unconsciously craves such containment because deep down he/she dreads the mental dissolution which results from such fragmentation and abiding chaos.

A riveting example of this phenomenon writ large is recorded in the Army–McCarthy Congressional Hearings, which occurred over a 3-month period from April to June, 1954.[7]

Attentive viewing of the most dramatic portions of the hearing,[8] demonstrating both the uncontained paranoia and the moments of its confrontation, may be mesmerizing. But, as well, this example shows that when the spell of the intense projections is broken, here by Counsel for the Army Welch's confrontational comments, how then the capacity for thinking minds to return is released and fear and dread can be replaced more by common sense and thought.

After World War II, Americans became very afraid of communism. Records suggest that infiltration of sympathizers did occur during and after the war. Joseph McCarthy, the junior senator from Wisconsin, became the spokesperson for this fear, and then became powerful as the chair of governmental committees aimed to rout out communists. The transcripts and videos reveal McCarthy functioning as a tyrant, amidst nearly paralyzing fear on the part of others. McCarthy seems to have slipped from an investigative role into an authoritarian position (illustrating Snyder's description of the rise of a tyrant). He may have capitalized on the country's fear to become the powerful figure who can set things right. With this increasing power he likely became increasingly authoritarian and thus unquestionable. At the time of these transcripts and videos McCarthy behaved as if any opposition to his investigations, even that of the President of the United States classifying documents away from his scrutiny, was colluding with communism.

The climactic point where confrontation begins to contain the tyranny occurred during the Army–McCarthy hearings, held in 1954, when Counsel for the Army Joseph Welch, a lawyer himself, confronted McCarthy with some false evidence he had presented the day before, but also and more specifically with how cruel McCarthy was being in his continuing insistence to try to label as a communist a young lawyer who Welch's team had carefully assessed. It seemed that McCarthy was actually retaliating against Welch's likely calling McCarthy's bluff a few minutes earlier when he, Welch, had demanded that the 138 names of communists purported by McCarthy's team to be in important military positions be presented "by sundown (today)." At this point, McCarthy then appears to attempt to divert attention by mentioning the young lawyer in Welch's law firm whom Welch had decided should not participate in the hearings because of a brief association with communism while in law school. Possibly he felt threatened not only by Welch's calling his bluff, but, as well, as Welch's revealing McCarthy's attempt to deceive the hearing with fabricated evidence. McCarthy, apparently still trying to hurt or divert Welch, continued to ask persistent questions about the young lawyer. Welch then loudly bursts out

> "Until this moment, Senator, I think I never really gauged your cruelty or your recklessness."[9]

McCarthy, who may be feeling he had hurt Welch, seemed to casually resume his attack on the young lawyer, at which point Welch angrily cut him short:

> "Senator, may we not drop this? We know he belonged to the Lawyer's Guild . . . Let us not assassinate this lad further, Senator; you've done enough. Have you no sense of decency, sir? At long last, have you left no sense of decency?"

In here, McCarthy appeared to gloat on Welch's discomfort and he continued to press about the young lawyer. And Welch then burst out:

> "I will discuss this no further . . . Mr. Chairman call the next witness." The chamber applauded.

It seemed that the spell of McCarthy as a powerful investigator, who should not be crossed, was broken. Senator Stuart Symington soon sparred with McCarthy and challenged him to take the oath and testify about some possible subversives in his own committee. McCarthy refused the challenge, saying Symington is out to undermine the fine work of his young men routing out communism. There is one more challenge by Symington, who exposed through questioning that the files in McCarthy's charge were not being carefully handled with regard to protecting classified data. The meeting was adjourned as the Senators were called out for a vote. McCarthy continued to rant, more or less to himself, that Symington was trying to smear his fine young men. By this time, it appeared in the video that no one was taking Joseph McCarthy seriously. Indeed, that McCarthy was talking only to himself as the chamber empties.

The observer of this video watches the descent of a powerful man used to making withering accusations, into a solitary, ranting figure locked onto a fixed idea. McCarthy's reputation plummeted as the American people viewed these hearings. In December, 1954, the U.S. Senate censured him. While he remained in office, during the next few months McCarthy's power essentially ceased. He experienced deteriorating health over the next four years and died in 1957, at the age of 48, likely due to the consequences of alcoholism.[10]

A view of the wider field allows one to reclaim a liberated mind which can offer a stabilizing perspective on the whole situation. When Joseph Welch, probably energized by rage, confronted McCarthy with his "cruelty and recklessness . . . have you no decency?" the spell was broken: minds in the room seem to be liberated from the tribal enslavement to a fixed idea of communists being everywhere, with McCarthy being the indomitable hunter in chief.

Another powerful example of this wider view, which offered a strengthened perspective, may be seen in closing remarks of the highly regarded journalist and war correspondent Edward R. Murrow ("See it Now" broadcast of March 9, 1954.)[11] His remarks offer context in terms of the country's fear of communism as an infiltrating and erosive force. Murrow, while acknowledging the need for investigation (one of Snyder's points) clearly contrasts investigation to the persecution of McCarthy's methods. A powerful aspect of Murrow's comments is his emphasis on the need for clarity and activity in searching out truths and responsible action on the part of thinking Americans as alternatives to fear. He implies the need not to submit to fear which can collapse the mind into accusation, submission and black and white thought. These words have relevance in contemporary times. As well, they clearly illustrate the liberating and orienting function of CARE.

McCarthy was given the opportunity for rebuttal and did so with a broadside attack upon Murrow, virtually accusing him on several fronts of communist sympathies. But he did not offer any corrections of the facts that Murrow had presented.[12]

In the episode following McCarthy's rebuttal, Murrow effectively squelched each of those accusations. He looked forward to the time when journalistic attention could be turned to issues other than the stirrings of the junior Senator from Wisconsin.[13]

Murrow's memorable remarks, "have no fear but keep your mind clear" were made in March, 1954. Joseph Welch's comments were made on June 9 of that year, and the Senate's censure was in December, 1954.

The transcript of Murrow's memorable commentary from March, 1954 may be accessed at https://www.youtube.com/watch?v=vEvEmkMNYHY. A summary is offered here as well, as an excellent example of nearly all the recommendations Snyder puts forth.

> the line between investigating and persecuting is a very fine one, and the junior Senator from Wisconsin has stepped over it repeatedly. His primary achievement has been in confusing the public mind . . . We must not confuse dissent with disloyalty . . . accusation is not proof . . . We will not be driven by fear into an age of unreason . . . we are not descended from men who feared to write, to speak, to associate and to defend causes that were, for the moment, unpopular.
>
> This is no time for men who oppose Senator McCarthy's methods to keep silent . . . We proclaim ourselves, as indeed we are, the defenders of freedom, wherever it continues to exist in the world, but we cannot defend freedom abroad by deserting it at home.
>
> The actions of the junior Senator from Wisconsin have caused alarm and dismay amongst our allies abroad and given considerable comfort to our enemies. And whose fault is that? Not really his. He didn't create this situation of fear; he merely exploited it—and rather successfully. Cassius was right: "The fault, dear Brutus, is not in our stars, but in ourselves."[14]

Edward R. Murrow's words beautifully illustrate nearly all the Lessons in Snyder's book about confronting tyranny: remain active, thoughtful, courageous, and patriotic in terms of whole-minded thought and universal ideals.

In an epilogue, historian Snyder describes two states of mind that he has observed from his understandings of history that threaten the clear-eyed vigilance needed to protect against tyranny. Both of these states represent descent of the thinking minds of a populace toward somnolence and sensory distraction. One state that he terms "the politics of inevitability" involves the partial retreat from thought: the assumption that the future will continue unchanging from the present seems to hypnotize the mind into minimizing attentive regard for the problems that might arise. The assumptions that globalization would continue indefinitely has mesmerized nations into becoming inattentive about the accruing inequality which inevitably accompanies assumptions of increasing inclusiveness.

The second state, which he terms "the politics of eternity," represents the total collapse of the thinking mind, the descent into sensory-based convictions including that of victimhood. Germany's descent into fascism and tyranny following World War I is one example. Contemporary American "politics of eternity" can be seen in the near paralysis of Congressional legislators more bent on polarization and tribal warfare than making policy. This situation, Snyder suggests, growing for decades as truth that has been sacrificed to opinion and emotional intensity, is being further fanned by the inflammatory efforts of a presidential leader bent on disruption rather than governance. When the mind collapses into a debris field, emotional reactivity replaces considered thought, excitement and outrage filling mental space. Such mental paralysis attracts the tyrant who promises to offer safety and order, and who then delivers terror and further mental enslavement of the mind or the nation too paralyzed to resist.

Snyder encourages the energetic mind to pay attention to history, and to learn, rather than to collapse into myth and mindless reactivity. As illustrated by Edward R. Murrow and Joseph Welch, I believe he is urging us to institute whole-minded thought, the courage to engage, to appreciate difference, and to include diversity in a wide-ranging discourse—all qualities embraced within the mental capacities we are defining as CARE.

Notes

1 Snyder (2017, p. 10).
2 Milgram (1974).
3 *Milgram Obedience Study with videos* (2011).
4 Haney, Banks, & Zimbardo (1973). Also, Zimbardo (2017).
5 The "arrests" by the Palo Alto police department and the khaki uniforms for the guards and shapeless prison garb for the prisoners would currently be recognized as priming the students toward their roles. Priming is now widely recognized in psychology as stimuli which significantly influence subsequent perception and experience. It appears to have been recognized in academic psychology in the late 1970s, several years after this prison experiment was conducted.
6 Haney, Banks, & Zimbardo (1973). Also, Zimbardo (2017).
7 The complete record of the hearings was published more than fifty years after the hearings in U.S. Senate See U.S. Senate. (1953–54).
     While there are several edited versions of the televised hearings available, United States Senate (1954). especially seems to offer context and fulsome coverage of the most dramatic proceedings, including Joseph Welch's famous confrontational question to McCarthy: ". . . have you no decency?"
8 U.S. Senate (1953–54) and Army McCarthy Hearings (2012) https://www.youtube.com/watch?v=wJHsur3HqcI.
9 U.S. Senate (1954).
10 Oshinsky (2005); Reeves (1982); Herman (2000).

11 *"See it Now"* broadcast March 9, 1954. These remarks may be viewed at Murrow (1954a).
12 McCarthy (1954) responds to Edward R. Murrow's previous report on April 6, 1954.
13 April 13 response of E. R. Murrow to McCarthy's attack. Murrow (1954c).
14 Murrow (1954d).

5

TRANSFORMATIONS VIA TRUST IN THE AS-YET UNKNOWABLE

In our efforts to guide the polarized mind toward integration, we have been tracing the unquenched fear, hatred and retaliation emanating from a culture based on the myth of white supremacy. These unmediated emotions led to upheaval in the cessation of slavery resulting from the American Civil War. That residual of the Old Southern culture was caught for generations after the War in entrenched grievance, being unable to mourn its losses and to face new realities. Instead, feeling frozen in grievance and the inability to mourn, this aspect of the South invoked vicious retaliations upon the former slaves, as an attempt to convince itself that it was somehow winning that civil war. This chapter offers a contrasting path for a culture facing catastrophic change, which may serve as a metaphor for a mind guided by moral principles based on respect and learning rather than shame, hate, and retaliation.

Jonathan Lear, distinguished professor of philosophy and psychoanalysis at the University of Chicago, describes the ethical underpinnings for the trust and hope that allowed the Crow nation in North America to survive the annihilation of their nomadic and warrior culture with dignity and honor. This involved a Crow chief's decision, foretold in a boyhood dream, for the tribe to learn from the white man, and to educate their children according to the white man's ways. Crucial here was the capacity to value learning from others, in this case, from the white man, without the collapse of the Crow's self-esteem and dignity. To be able to value learning and to embrace new cultural and personal identities differs considerably from what the entrenched culture of the Old South could do for generations, both before and after the Civil War.

The South we are considering could not bear to face the potential catastrophe of cultural change given its adherence to shame-based honor. In contrast, the Crow nation was capable of relinquishing its previous culture and identity, due to an underlying ethic of honor based on self-respect and the capacity to trust in the unknown. The Crow ethic allows more flexibility, trust and hope than the ethic of Southern honor. The Crow ethic exemplifies the emotional integration needed for emergence from fragmented mental states. This is an ethic worth keeping in mind as we face current turbulence.

Jonathan Lear has written a compelling book, *Radical Hope: Ethics in the Face of Cultural Devastation.*[1] His saga orbits around the Crow chief, generally known as Plenty Coups ("Many Achievements"). The Crow people had lived for generations as a nomadic, buffalo-hunting and warrior society on the plains of North America. For several decades the tribe had felt increasing pressure from their mortal enemies the Sioux. With this constant threat, their leaders felt that alliance with the white man would protect against potential deadly encounters with their long-time enemies. This ongoing risk of tribal obliteration, which was not uncommon among the plains Indians, is important in terms of the sense of immanent catastrophe being part of tribal anxieties. It also offers some context for Plenty Coups' childhood dream, which became pivotal in terms of the future direction for his tribe.

Plenty Coups, then, at 9 years of age, had a dream which spelled the end of the buffalo way of life: the dreamer is shown a hole in the ground into which all the buffalo disappear and from that hole spotted buffalo (the white man's cattle) emerge to cover the plains. This part of the dream is clear: the buffalo would disappear within Plenty Coups' lifetime, leading the tribe to ally with the white man, which the dream suggests was the wave of the future. But the next part of the dream needed the interpretation of Yellow Bear, one of the elders of the tribe. This part of the dream involves a huge storm that destroys all the trees except that of the chickadee, the little bird which listens and learns from others. This interpretation suggested that the tribe would need to change, and to focus on learning, adapting in mind as well as body. While it was not uncommon for elders to interpret the enigmatic aspects of their young men's dreams, it is also interesting to consider that an elder was needed for this interpretation because the drastic change foretold would be too painful and frightening an aspect of reality for anyone less esteemed to interpret in a way that could be accepted by the tribe.

An important element here is the relation the Crow had to dream phenomena: typically, the young men, often boys, would go into the wilderness in order to dream and the older men of the tribe would then interpret the dreams they brought back. The Crow felt that these dreams emerged from the deeply revered spirit world and thus deserved to be trusted, even though the people themselves might not fully know what the dreams foretold. This suggests that the Crow, as a people, could trust that the messages from the spirit world were truth-telling about the as-yet unknown future. From a psychoanalytic perspective, one's world-view may include the expectation of hope versus dread that reflects one's level of internal trust and well-being. Mental and emotional integration proposes that the farther one strays from self-respect, the more dread one experiences in conscious life and in dreams. Faith in the unknown future (whether guided by dreams from the spirit world for the Crow, or intuitions based on living a self-respecting life for us) suggest that an ethic based on inner truth and courage offers the promise for survival, and perhaps thriving beyond the abyss of the unknown.

The Crow tribe lived on the edge of danger in terms of threats from other tribes. The constant threat of annihilation was something the Crow lived with, so there was no great surprise at the dream of the disappearance of the familiar way of life (the buffalo) to be replaced by the unfamiliar (the white man's "spotted buffalo"). Lear also suggests that with the tribe's future in jeopardy they might turn to the dream for signs of what was to come.[2] While Plenty Coups' dream could be considered as a thought that could not yet be known,[3] the dream, taken seriously by the tribe, might also offer a way to contemplate their future. That is, to think and to make practical plans as far as was possible.[4]

Further, the chickadee was considered to be a curious, observant little bird who could learn and adapt. The dream representation might suggest the need to be similarly open to, and learn from the wisdom of others.[5] While it may not be clear what would comprise wisdom in the midst of cultural catastrophe, learning in a way that would foster individual and cultural emergence in some form would seem to be part of the quality of this new virtue. Perhaps overly condensing Lear's elegant discussion, which calls upon various ancient and modern philosophers' views of ethics, I believe he suggests that Plenty Coups' capacity to value the dream figures as serving the functions of respect-worthy internal guidance, is vital. The dreamer, being told to emulate the chickadee's openness to learn,[6] exemplifies the representation of flexible learning as an honorable replacement for the more traditional guidelines toward courage as a hunter or a warrior. New sources of honor, then, based on learning and adaptability to changing circumstances seem pivotal in this remarkable saga.

Lear argues that sustaining sources of courage underlie the capacity for Radical Hope. That is, hope that bridges the chasm of the unknown derives from trust in and development of one's basic, innate capacities.[7] He suggests that Plenty Coups valued the dream as a window into his interior, but also the dream as an imaginative exploration in problem-solving. Curiosity and learning, then, become adaptive modes for an unknown future. Lear can be read as emphasizing an ethic which guides one to live according to abiding self-respect, which values not only one's own capacities and judgment but also provides a sense of harmony with one's internal and external world. These values and lessons could also guide communities and nations, in Plenty Coups' time as well as in our own.

Lear suggests that this transcendent hope, deeply rooted in a sense of goodness and respect, harkens back to infancy with dependence upon the goodness of providing parental figures. This formulation, similar to the anticipation of CARE, is considered here as a fundamental source for emergence and integration.

All myths are the products of imagination and mental projections: e.g. the myth of white supremacy, and the myth of the chickadee as a curious bird who can learn from others. We tend to populate the external world we live in with our perceptions and assumptions about the nature of things. As the poet Wordsworth, and others have noted "'we half create' and half perceive the world we inhabit."[8]

What then demarcates the projections of Plenty Coups from those of the Southerners who subscribed to, and built, a culture upon the myth of white supremacy? Why should one be valued over the other? Perhaps the answer is whether the myths contain distortions of reality. The myth of white supremacy was created to foster a myth of white superiority while also allowing the white slavers to justify not only enslaving the blacks, but also treating them in inhuman ways. The blacks as property, so the myth contends, may be dealt with without much moral compunction. A deeper distortion of reality might be considered as well: internally, every white slaver must have been at least mildly terrified about anticipated retaliation from the slaves he abused. The slaves were physically stronger and, in many cases, more numerous than the whites on the plantations. In addition, the mechanisms of splitting and projection inform us that when we abandon whole-minded functioning we automatically condemn ourselves to the mental world of fragmentation.

Thus, our projections haunt and indeed enslave us: we often blame and often punish others for the very impulses and thoughts that we ourselves cannot bear to realize as our own. We are terrified about the repatriation of these projections as retaliations from brutalized slaves, or retributions from our own shames and guilts. We may also be as terrified of the pain of facing and owning these disavowed aspects as parts of ourselves, pains which we must suffer if we are to become whole-minded once more.

On the other hand, myths, such as the curious chickadee capable of learning from others, represent aspirations toward flexibility, adaptability and whole-minded functioning. The myth of the chickadee encourages openness and trust toward the wider reality, rather than clinging to stasis out of fear of an unknown future. Such myths foster growth and integration at the level of the individual and the community.

A compelling vignette illustrates Plenty Coups' dignity and capacity for mourning as an individual and as a representative of his tribe. The alliance he formed commanded the respect of the white man to such a degree that he was invited to represent all the Native American Nations at the ceremony for the World War I Unknown Soldier in Arlington Cemetery in 1921. *The New York Times* report (with a variation in spelling) notes Plenty Coups' participation:

> When the aged Indian, with finely chiseled profile, removed his own feathered war bonnet and placed it tenderly on the marble edge of the sarcophagus and then lifted his arms in supplication toward Heaven, it constituted one of the outstanding features of the whole remarkable ceremony. Many Indians served in the American forces in the World War, and General Foch has paid them high tribute. When Chief Plenty Coos (*New York Times'* spelling) deposited the war bonnet today he acted in the name of all American Indians.[9]

This dignified laying to rest of the insignias of the Crow's past culture was a demonstration of respect for self and others. It is not difficult to see how he shone as a charismatic leader of his nation.[10] The vignette offers contrast to former arch enemy Chief Sitting Bull's position. Sitting Bull maintained that collaborating with the enemy was selling one's soul. He may be seen as informed by honor based on the unchanging assumption of the white man as the enemy forever. This might be similar to loyalty to the myth of white supremacy, an attitude shaped by splitting and polarization, which continues to shape the attitudes of many Americans.

While contemporary America has viewed itself, in most ways, as an ascending culture, thinking about this significant gesture of Plenty Coups is instructional. It gives us the space and metaphor for individual recognition and mourning amidst dignity and respect. That is, change without collapse and trust without knowing what the future holds. These are the very qualities required in the rescue of our minds embattled by narrow definitions of who we are and what we know.

Notes

1 Lear (2006).
2 *Ibid.*, p. 76.
3 *Ibid.*
4 *Ibid.*, p. 78.
5 *Ibid.*, pp. 82–82.
6 *Ibid.*, p. 90.
7 *Ibid.*, p. 126.
8 McGilchrist (2009), p. 369.
9 "100,000 Gathered in Arlington Hills," *The New York Times*, November 12, 1921. Also quoted in Stewart (1921).
10 A reminder to the reader of the notation in group phenomena of the importance of the charismatic leader to the survival of the group. Plenty Coups, as a charismatic leader, led his tribe toward the transformation to a new culture based on alliance with the white man. He did this with dignity and respect for self and other, and thus did not abandon or feel abandoned by his nation.

6

APPRECIATING THE PAIN OF INTEGRATION

European reflections

Adding to this meditation on the elements which re-integrate the personality, Rob Riemen, a contemporary Dutch cultural philosopher, adds to this modern philosophical discussion.[1] He notes the inevitable roots of fascism which plague the modern mind, and he defines fascism as "the political cultivation of our worst irrational sentiments: resentment, hatred, xenophobia, lust for power and fear."[2] Quoting Federico Fellini "Fascism always arises from a provincial spirit, a lack of knowledge of real problems and people's refusal – through laziness, prejudice, greed, or arrogance to give their lives deeper meaning."[3] Fascism, which emerged from populist uprisings, promises to "make (us) great again" in offering the power and the false promise to return to a past which never really existed.[4] These observations echo those of Timothy Snyder's study of tyranny.

A truly democratic civilization, Riemen notes, relies on the "human capacity to transcend ourselves, to have imagination and empathy, and to live in truth, create beauty, and do justice,"[5] while countering the superficial appearances of culture, including cynicism and resentment. These thoughts are reminiscent of Lear's notations about Plenty Coups' qualities: his trust in learning from the white man rather than following Sitting Bull's view that allying with the white man was a cowardly betrayal of the dictate to hold him as the enemy forever.

Citing several astute observers, including de Tocqueville in 1830s America, and later Nietzsche in 1870s Europe, Riemen states that as men emerge from tyranny democracy becomes possible. But rather than hold as beacons the values which transcend the self, such as beauty, honesty, generosity, and truth, the newly freed populace appears, from these observations, to lower their view and to indulge in sensory pleasures and momentary excitement and entertainment. That is, there is a tendency to become fully occupied with sensory distractions, without regard to higher ideals. The attendant vacancy of spirit, Riemen holds, is the fount of fascism. He cites ignorance as the main reason for fascism. By ignorance, Riemen means giving into our base emotions – greed, lust, power, envy – rather than engaging in the constraints of self-control, and self-respect, guided by the liberal ideals of truth, justice, and beauty.

This reluctance to see beyond the self in terms of higher ideals has other consequences, Riemen reminds us. He quotes Paul Valery[6] who in the 1920s suggested that there is a vulnerability in the move toward democracy to pervert equality in the demand that everything should be made easily available to the every-day mind. That is, so no one has to be made to feel uncomfortable. This kind of "equality" may discourage one from striving to attain understanding, to learn difficult lessons, or to suffer pain and frustration. Such a lack of rigorous instruction in exercising thought and valuing difference can lead to resentment at the frustrations encountered by the uneducated mind. This, Riemen contends, is the fuel for fascism, because there are really no deeper ideologies within fascism beyond fanning the flames of sensory-based resentment.

These warnings have relevance in contemporary times. They illustrate the liberating and orienting function of the CARE-bringing mind, capable of receiving and bearing current divisive fears and terrors. This wider-ranging mind can also realize that various realities may pertain at the same time. It can bear to empathically suffer, including the pain of accountability, vital for the transformation of the polarized view into one of many potential views, rather than all of reality. This rescuing state of mind, then, ferries the journey from the realities based on power to those based on humanity.

But Riemen would add, with European boldness of thought, the importance of ignorance and the resentment that thinking may require mental disturbance. Our on-going study of splitting and projection demonstrates that viewing the humanity-based other, who can value these higher ideals, might, indeed, fuel envy and hatred of that humanity, now seen via projection, to be arrogantly looking down on the "stupidity" of the more sensory-oriented self.

Riemen concludes that the most significant antidote to the descent into fascism is the maintenance of the humanities and aesthetics in our culture. Our education based around those ideals, such as beauty, generosity, truth, justice, and empathy, inspire and guide us. He cites Spinoza, the 17th century humanist, who maintained that man is truly free from the enslavement of ignorance when he can reach toward those ideals.[7] Only then is he free from the entrapment which base emotions may otherwise bestow.

Some further American thoughts

During the first weeks after the 2016 election, *The New Yorker* magazine published several democratically leaning authors' responses to the election of Donald Trump.[8] The following are two excerpts from this selection of authors.

Historian Jill Lepore writes: "(The 2016 election) . . . ends an era of American idealism . . . 'The fate of the greatest of all modern Republics trembles in the balance,' Frederick Douglass said in a speech he gave in Philadelphia, in 1862.[9] Born into slavery, Douglass had escaped in 1838. What astonished him, as the Civil War raged, was how blind Americans were to its origins . . . Douglass blamed slavery: 'We have sought to bind the chains of slavery on the limbs of the black man, without thinking that at last we should find the other end of that hateful chain about our own necks.'"

Lepore continues: "But the deepest reason (for our current troubles) is inequality: the forms of political, cultural, and economic polarization that have been widening, not narrowing, for decades. Inequality, like slavery, is a chain that binds at both ends."

> For Douglass, the aftermath of the fight to end slavery was a lesson about the persistence of inequality . . .
>
> Trump was elected because he got something right, about the suffering of Americans, and about the arrogance of politicians, of academics, and of the press. What he got wrong can be proved only by the forces of humility, of clarity, and of honesty. When does an ending begin? Douglass saw that the end of a republic begins on the day when the heroism of the struggle for equality yields to the cowardice of resentment.[10]

Here, "the heroism of the struggle" would likely include the discomforts created by the doubt and uncertainty that inevitably accompany strife and the daring to be open to change. And Douglass' phrase "the cowardice of resentment" may be thought of as the emotional withdrawal into bitterness, when one has projected away one's authority and willingness to persist and struggle and suffer the pains that embracing equality might entail. Embracing equality as well, means respecting one another, even if views differ significantly, rather than withdrawing into the bunkered, polarizing state of mind which views the other as an ignorant or arrogant enemy. Basically, here, we are considering how powerful and painful it may be to re-unite the mind after it has been cleaved into polarized positions.

The second offering from this *New Yorker* article restates the themes of heroism, hope and faith. Noted author Junot Diaz begins with the courage to deeply feel pain and to mourn.

> So, what now? Well, first and foremost, we need to <u>feel</u>. We need to connect courageously with the rejection, the fear, the vulnerability that Trump's victory has inflicted on us, without turning away or numbing ourselves or lapsing into cynicism. We need to bear witness to what we have lost: our safety, our sense of belonging, our vision of our country. We need to <u>mourn</u> all these injuries fully, so that they do not drag us into despair, so repair will be possible.
>
> And while we're doing the hard, necessary work of mourning, we should avail ourselves of the old formations that have seen us through darkness.[11] (emphasis in the original)

Diaz urges organizing to be heard and to appreciate the hard work of previous generations of slaves and lowly workers whose combined efforts have "transformed the universe."

He continues by invoking hope:

> But all the fighting in the world will not help us if we do not also <u>hope</u> . . . not blind optimism but what the philosopher Jonathan Lear calls radical hope. 'What makes this hope radical,' Lear writes, 'is that it is directed toward a future goodness that transcends the current ability to understand what it is.' Radical hope is not so much something you have but something you practice; it demands flexibility, openness, and what Lear describes as 'imaginative excellence'. Radical hope is our best weapon against despair, even when despair seems justifiable; it makes the survival of the end of your world possible. Only radical hope could have imagined people like us into existence. And I believe

that it will help us create a better, more loving future.[12] (emphasis in the original)

Here Diaz cites Lear's hope beyond what one can imagine at the moment. Faith in the future, rather than sinking into a cynicism which might reduce the space for hope into barren meaninglessness. This may also be thought of as faith in the long-term arc of history beyond what we can know or predict. The compass of striving amidst hope rather than cynicism and hate will set a trajectory which will abide by the ideals of justice and truth. Radical hope, based on reverence for beauty and truth, then, may offer the possibility for transformation and thus rescue of the embattled mind.

Riemen embraces aesthetic ideals; Lepore recognizes inequality with humility and honesty and Diaz mourns, but also moves forward with hope. These authors, along with others mentioned throughout the previous chapters, offer guiding beacons toward rescue of the mind distracted by sensory intensities and fractured in order to avoid painful truths.

The enslaved mind of the white supremacist Southerner is a useful metaphor for the potential enslavement of our beleaguered minds. Rescue involving the re-integration of the mind means facing painful, warded-off truths with openness and humility. It also means constraining oneself from the distractions of gossip and outrage. Maintaining transcendent ideals, such as truth and beauty, as beacons may help one to refrain from the cynical allure of grievance and resentment. Both of the latter can foreclose the possibility of further thought in preference to indulging in the conviction of meaninglessness, hopelessness and stasis. Such confrontations with oneself, guided by the ideals mentioned, offer soft-edged but deep-going experience, which develops quiet inner space. True rescue seems to involve the inspirations that emanate from this inner space.

Notes

1 Riemen (2018).
2 *Ibid.*, p. 21.
3 *Ibid.*, p. 25.
4 *Ibid.*, p. 26.
5 *Ibid.*
6 *Ibid.*, pp. 43–45, 47–49, 53–55. Actually, within this opening chapter, Riemen quotes several noted contemporary authors about the dangers of lassitude, resentment and indulgence: in pages 47–49 he cites Max Scheler's emphasis on how resentment degrades values in a culture in his 1912 work *The Resentment in the Construction of Moralitie* ; in pages 43–45 Riemen cites Ortega y Gasset's warning

in his 1932 book *The Revolt of the Masses* that such degradation dangerously erodes Europe's morals. In pages 53–55 he cites the warning of Menno ter Braak in his 1937 essay "National socialism as a doctrine of Resentment" that fascism just inflames resentment, having nothing more to offer.

7 *Ibid.*, p. 38.
8 Lepore (2016); Diaz (2016).
9 Douglass (1862).
10 *Ibid.*, pp. 59–60.
11 *Ibid.*, p. 65.
12 *Ibid.*

7

SUMMARY REFLECTIONS

We began with a question, whether we as a nation, or perhaps the Western world, are nearing a cultural shift from entrenched polarization toward openness to diversity and the welcoming of difference. We have considered white supremacy in the United States as a model for a persistent polarizing myth, now centuries old. We have also looked closely at universal mental mechanisms which have bolstered this myth.

In so doing, we have noted that the products of our self-reflection may be disturbing because some aspects of our human nature are not pleasant to consider. In addition, our wish for ease and comfort may far outweigh curious urges to explore ourselves as well as other unknown realms.

But, we have also seen that in settling for simpler choices, we are nearly always changing mental worlds. That is, we revert to earlier modes of functioning, going from a sense of potential wide-ranging thought and secure inner authority to a sense of having no agency and possibly no sense of interiority. In this state we experience our authority as being firmly lodged in another, while our narrowed view sees the world in black and white terms—us and them, good and evil. This tribal state of mind may serve us when there is a need for one leader and for group cohesion. An external authority is appealing because the individual is then not burdened by personal responsibility with its attendant doubt. Further, loyalty to the group fosters an action-based posture, convinced that its point of view is honorable and even patriotic.

But the reversion to simpler realities does violence to the more whole-minded self. The mechanisms of splitting and projection cleave away the most highly evolved mental capacities that foster appreciation of the nuances, ambiguities and the grays of complex reality. Reversion to ancient tribal modes re-engage the polarized myth of idealized goodness about oneself and one's kin, and a feared and dangerous other, which has been created by the projection of disavowed disturbances. These external targets, now felt to be threats to well-being, must be carefully controlled or subjugated. Any new or different ideas about reality would be felt as jarring and alien, especially if it were to reveal the myths as just that, myths, instead of unquestioned truths to live by. It may seem ironic that a would-be protective mechanism (splitting) for the early growing mind can also re-create the mental world of danger and polarization, one crying out for tribal unity and defensive power-based tactics as the only source of regulation that this state of mind can appreciate.

Rescue from this polarized entrenchment involves the capacities to withstand the destabilization of shifting mental worlds. The sturdy, compassionate function of CARE is described as providing the needed capacities to face disavowed truths, along with the capacities to absorb the pains, rages and chaos incumbent in reintegrating the fractured mind.

Citing some details, about how the dissolution of the self leads to our descent from humanity to inhumanity: Milgram's experiments in the 1960s demonstrate how easily we may lose our moral compass when in the presence of a seemingly significant external authority. Zimbardo's prison experiments further illustrate not only that rapid loss of identity which occurs when one becomes defined by an assigned role, but also how imprisoning and dehumanizing these roles may become.

Timothy Snyder's description of the rise of a tyrant suggests that an individual capitalizing on the fear within a populace can take on the role of an increasingly authoritarian figure, who convinces himself and others that he alone can make things better. Joseph McCarthy illustrated this tendency in 1950s America, while the confrontations by Joseph Welch and Edward R. Murrow illustrate how a clearly thinking mind can confront and unmask the tyrannical mentality in a manner which restores the humanizing function of whole-minded thought. Welch's confrontation brought the humanity, and Murrow's discussion demonstrated how searching out truths and responsible action are potent alternatives to the dissolution into fear.

Further, rescue toward whole-mindedness seems to involve trust and faith beyond what can be immediately known. Jonathan Lear offers the illustration of the Crow Indian Chief Plenty Coups' radical hope and how it guided his people through cultural catastrophe as they faced being overrun by the unceasing encroachment of the white man. This guidance was based on deep respect for self and other and for the wisdom of one's dreams as messages from the ancestral spirit world, what moderns might think of as implicit, experience-based intuition. The deepest lessons here were how this self-respect may guide learning from, rather than automatically fighting with the other: a potent suggestion that trust based in self-respect may aid in the capacity for faith in the unknowable future.

The contemporary European philosophical voice of Rob Riemen adds to the understanding that the reversion to tribal states of mind easily leads to the rise of fascism. He defines fascism as the cultivation of resentment and hatred, which arise out of laziness, greed and arrogance, states of mind that refuse to give life deeper meaning. Citing observations of Americans in the 1830s and of Europeans 150 years later, he notes how once external tyranny wanes populations seem reticent as individuals to adopt the internal authority and responsibility needed to maintain true freedom of thought by combatting the ignorance that abides in sensory-based, self-indulgent mental states. True freedom, he contends, involves the ongoing effort, aided by transcendent values, to strive for meaning, depth and self-respect.

And finally, in our survey of the qualities of CARE we cite modern historian Jill Lepore's emphasis on the need to recognize inequality with honesty and humility, and Junot Diaz' echo of Jonathon Lear's urging about the need to mourn but also to move forward with hope. These authors, along with others mentioned throughout the previous chapters, offer guiding beacons toward rescue for the mind distracted by sensory intensities and fractured in order to avoid painful truths.

Overarching themes presented in this book involve the realization that facing the pain of mental integration[1] and striving for truth and meaning amidst respect for self and other fosters the evolution of our humanity. While our slackening efforts out of laziness, greed, and the hatred of painful reality inevitably leads to our descent as individuals and nations from potential freedom of thought and trust in the future into the entrapments of our devolving inhumanity.

Note

1 Chapter 2, Endnote #3 refers to an excerpt about the dread of mental and emotional reintegration. As mentioned there, reintegration is so at the heart of this book, that it is excerpted once again in this final Endnote:

Reintegration involves the repatriation of . . . (externalized) disturbance as part of self. This process means realizing that not only the obstructing disturbances, but also the divisive forces that aim to disown the disturbances, are not external. Such recognition indeed annihilates the myth of being the power at the centre of the world and re-establishes the humbler processive to and fro involved in learning. In lived experience this clear view and dismantling of . . . (the hard shell of certainty) is not a gentle process. It is one that involves bearing pain and tension as one softens the hardened carapace, risking feeling humiliated, as one owns the disavowed elements, before feeling the relief of reunion. In the lived moment, that pain and tension involve the risk of embracing need, which has been felt as weakness, trust taking the place of cynicism, attentive care seen as other than manipulation or domination. As mentioned, this reunification process may involve a jarring and then dis-arming shift from power to the wider awareness of vulnerability and need, as humiliation trends toward humility. (Anderson (2016), pp. 91–92)

REFERENCES

Alexander, M. (2010, 2012). *The New Jim Crow: Mass Incarceration in the Age of Colorblindness*. New York: The New Press.

Anderson, C. (2016). *White Rage: The Unspoken Truth of Our Racial Divide*. New York: Bloomsbury.

Anderson, C. (2017). The Policies of White Resentment. *The New York Times*. https:// www.nytimes.com/2017/08/05/opinion/sunday/white-resentment-affirmative -action.html [Accessed August 6, 2017].

Anderson, M. (2016). *The Wisdom of Lived Experience*. London: Karnac.

Arendt, H. (1958). *The Origins of Totalitarianism*. Revised edition. Cleveland, OH: Meridian.

Arendt, H. (2003). *Responsibility and Judgment*. New York: Schoken.

Army McCarthy Hearings. (2012). https://www.youtube.com/watch?v=wJHsur3 HqcI [Accessed July 14, 2018].

Ayers, E. (2003). *In the Presence of Mine Enemies*. New York: Norton.

Baldwin, J. (1965). James Baldwin Debates William F. Buckley. YouTube. www. youtube.com/watch?v=oFeoS41xe7w [Accessed May 28, 2018].

Barbaro, M. (2017a). The Daily Podcast. *The New York Times*. October 18, 2017. Available at www.nytimes.com [Accessed October 18, 2017].

Barbaro, M. (2017b). The Daily Podcast. *The New York Times*. August 22, 2017. Available at www.nytimes.com [Accessed March 17, 2018].

Baumeister, R., Finkenauer, K., & Vohs, K. (2001). Bad is stronger than good. *Review of General Psychology*. 5(4):323–370.

BBC News. (2017). Boston March against Right-Wing Rally Draws Thousands. www.bbc.com/news/world-us-canada-40980175 [Accessed March 18, 2018].

Beinart, P. (2016). Why America Is Moving Left. *The Atlantic*. www.theatlantic.com/

magazine/archive/2016/01/why-america-is-moving-left/419112/ [Accessed May 28, 2018].

Bion, W. (1962). The Psycho-Analytic Study of Thinking. *International Journal of Psycho-Analysis.* 43:306–310.

Bolte Taylor, J. (2008a). *My Stroke of Insight.* London: Hodder & Stoughton.

Bolte Taylor, J. (2008b). "Jill Bolte Taylor's Stroke of Insight," February 2008. TED podcast. https://www.ted.com/talks/jill_bolte_taylor_s_powerful_stroke_of_in sight [Accessed November 3, 2015].

Brooks, D. (2016). The Power of the Dinner Table. *The New York Times.* www.ny times.com/2016/10/18/opinion/the-power-of-a-dinner-table.html?action= click&pgtype=Homepage&clickSource=story-heading&module=opinion-c-col-left-region&region=opinion-c-col-left-region&WT.nav=opinion-c-col-left-region [Accessed September 6, 2017].

Buckner, R. L., Andrews-Hanna J. R., & Schacter, D. L. (2008). The Brain's Default Network: Anatomy, Function, and Relevance to Disease. *Annals of the New York Academy of Sciences.* March, 1124:1–38.

Cash, W. (1941). *The Mind of the South.* New York: Vintage Books.

Civitarese, G. (2011). Exploring Core Concepts: Sexuality, Dreams and the Unconscious. *International Journal of Psycho-Analysis.* 92(2):277–280.

Covington, C. (2012). Hannah Arendt, Evil and the Eradication of Thought. *International Journal of Psycho-Analysis.* 93(5):1215–1236.

Daily Kos. (2012). An Open Letter to the People Who Hate Obama More than They Love America. https://www.dailykos.com/stories/2012/1/9/1053088/- [Accessed August 14, 2017].

Deyle, S. (2005). *Carry Me Back: The Domestic Slave Trade In American Life.* New York: Oxford, p. 179.

Diaz, J. (2016). "Radical Hope" in Aftermath: Responses to the Election of Dona's J. Trump. *The New Yorker,* November 21, 2016, p. 65.

Dickson, Mary Frances Warren "Mollie." (1864). Private diary of young Missouri schoolteacher, now at Museum of the Rockies, Bozeman, Montana.

Donald, D. (1981). "A Generation of Defeat." In Walter J. Fraser, Jr. and Winifred B. Moore, Jr. (Eds.), *From the Old South to the New.* Westport, CT: Greenwood Press.

Douglass, F. (1862). *The Reasons for Our Troubles.* http://rbscp.lib.rochester.edu/4381 [Accessed March 17, 2018].

Douglass, F. and others. (1853). *Proceedings of the Colored National Convention.* Rochester, NY: Printed at the office of Frederick Douglass' Papers, p. 137. http://coloredconventions.org/files/original/b1c49afd97f0dbc8358896c21a92ae05.pdf [Accessed January 29, 2018].

Dubenko, A. (2017). Right and Left on the Violence in Charlottesville. *The New York Times.* www.nytimes.com/2017/08/14/us/politics/trump-charlottesville-left-right-react.html [Accessed May 28, 2018].

Durkheim, E. (1915, 1965). *The Elementary Forms of Religious Life.* New York: The Free Press.

Effron, D. (2018). Why Trump Supporters Don't Mind His Lies. *New York Times.* https://www.nytimes.com/2018/04/28/opinion/sunday/why-trump-support ers-dont-mind-his-lies.html?action=click&pgtype=Homepage&clickSource= story-heading&module=opinion-c-col-right-region&region=opinion-c-col-right-region&WT.nav=opinion-c-col-right-region [Last Accessed April 29, 2018].

Ellis, R. (2017). The KKK Rally in Charlottesville was Outnumbered by Counterprotesters. *CNN.* https://www.cnn.com/2017/07/08/us/kkk-rally-char lottesville-statues/index.html [Accessed March 17, 2018].

Ferenczi, S. (1988). *The Clinical Diary of Sandor Ferenczi,* ed. J. Dupond. Cambridge, MA: Harvard University Press.

Friston, K. (2010). The Free-Energy Principle: A Unified Brain Theory? *Nature Reviews Neuroscience.* 11:127–138.

Fuster, J. (2001). The Prefrontal Cortex—An Update: Time Is of the Essence. *Neuron.* www.sciencedirect.com/science/article/pii/S0896627301002859 [Accessed October 29, 2017].

Gasset, O. (1932). *The Revolt of the Masses.* New York: Norton.

Gilmore, J. (1864). Our Visit to Richmond. *The Atlantic Monthly.* September, 1864, pp. 338–357. https://loa-shared.s3.amazonaws.com/static/pdf/Gilmore_Visit_Richmond.pdf [Accessed November 5, 2017].

Goodwin, D. (2005). *Team of Rivals: The Political Genius of Abraham Lincoln.* New York: Simon & Schuster, pp. 77–79.

Gorman, S., & Gorman, J. (2017). *Denying to the Grave: Why We Ignore the Facts that Will Save Us.* New York: Oxford University Press.

Gurevich, H. (2008). The Language of Absence. *International Journal of Psychoanalysis.* 89:561–578.

Haney, C., Banks, C., & Zimbardo, P. (1973). A Study of Prisoners and Guards in a Simulated Prison. *Naval Research Reviews.* www.zimbardo.com/down loads/1973%20A%20Study%20of%20Prisoners%20and%20Guards,%20Naval %20Research%20Reviews.pdf [Accessed October 18, 2017].

Haskell, D. (2017). *The Songs of Trees: Stories from Nature's Great Connectors.* New York: Viking.

Herman, A. (2000). *Joseph McCarthy: Reexamining the Life and Legacy of America's Most Hated Senator.* New York: Free Press.

Hertz, N. (2013). *Eyes Wide Open: How to Make Smart Decisions in a Confusing World.* New York: HarperCollins.

Hochschild, A. R. (2016). *Strangers in Their Own Land: Anger and Mourning on the American Right.* New York: The New Press.

Huddy, L., Mason, L., & Aaroe, L. (2015). Expressive Partisanship: Campaign Involvement, Political Emotion, and Partisan Identity. *American Political Science Review.* https://www.cambridge.org/core/journals/american-political-science-review/article/expressive-partisanship-campaign-involvement-political-emotion-and-partisan-identity/7D2A2C87FBEBBE5DABAAF9658B3162AA [Accessed October 27, 2017].

Hunt, A., & Wheeler, B. (2018). Brexit: All You Need to Know about the UK Leaving the EU. *BBC News*. www.bbc.com/news/uk-politics-32810887 [Accessed May 28, 2018].

Isenberg, N. (2016). *White Trash: The 400 Year Untold History of Class in America*. New York: Viking.

Iyengar, S., Sood, G., & Lelkes, Y. (2012). Affect, Not Ideology: A Social Identity Perspective on Polarization. *Public Opinion Quarterly*. 76(3):405–431.

Kalichman, S. (2009). *Denying AIDS: Conspiracy Theories, Pseudoscience, and Human Tragedy*. New York: Copernicus.

Kanouse, D., & Hanson, L. (1972). "Negativity in Evaluations." In E. E. Jones, D. E. Kanouse, S. Valins, H. H. Kelley, R. E. Nisbett, & B. Weiner (Eds.), *Attribution: Perceiving the Causes of Behavior*. Morristown, NJ: General Learning Press.

Kaplan-Solms, K., & Solms, M. (2000). *Clinical Studies in Neuro-Psychoanalysis: Introduction to a Depth Neuropsychology*. London: Karnac.

Kaufman, J., Yang, B. X., Douglas-Palumberi, H., Houshyar, S. Lipschitz, D., Kristal, J. H., & Gelenter, J. (2004). Social Supports and Serotonin Transporter Gene Moderate Depression in Maltreated Children. *Proceedings of the National Academy of Sciences*. 101(49):17316–17321.

Lear, J. (2006). *Radical Hope: Ethics in the Face of Cultural Devastation*. Cambridge, MA: Harvard Press.

Lepore, J. (2016). "Wars Within," in Aftermath: Responses to the Election of Donald J. Trump. *The New Yorker*, November 21, 2016. pp. 59–60.

Lincoln, D. (2015). *Einstein's True Biggest Blunder*. https://www.space.com/31055-removing-cosmological-constant-was-the-blunder.html [Accessed January 13 2018].

Lopez, G. (2018). How the NRA Resurrected the Second Amendment. *Vox*, October 12, 2017; updated May 4, 2018. https://www.vox.com/policy-and-politics/2017/10/12/16418524/nra-second-amendment-guns-violence.

Lumpkin, K. (1991). *The Making of a Southerner* (1946; reprint, Athens: University of Georgia Press.

McCarthy, J. (1954). *Joseph McCarthy Responds to Edward R. Murrow's Previous Report on "See It Now."* (1954). www.youtube.com/watch?v=MnKTgmOJr78 [Accessed May 28, 2017].

McGilchrist, I. (2009). *The Master and his Emissary*. New Haven, CT: Yale University Press.

Mackintosh, E. (2017). Europe's Migrant Crisis Isn't Going Away, but It Is Changing. *CNN*. www.cnn.com/2017/08/17/europe/mediterranean-migrant-crisis-2017/index.html [Accessed May 28, 2018].

Maiello, S. (2000). Broken Links: Attack or Breakdown? Notes on the Origins of Violence. *Journal of Child Psychotherapy*. 26:5–24.

Mancia, M. (1981). On the Beginning of Mental Life in the Foetus. *International Journal of Psychoanalysis*. 62:351–357.

Marcolini, B., & Decker, B. (2017). Violence in Charlottesville. *The New York Times*. https://www.nytimes.com/video/us/100000005363670/charlottesville-virginia-white-nationalist-protests.html [Accessed September 20, 2017].

Milgram Obedience Study with Videos of Some of the Actual Participants in the Original Experiments. (2011). https://www.youtube.com/watch?v=fCVlI-_4G ZQ [Accessed December 12, 2017].

Milgram, S. (1974). *Obedience to Authority: An Experimental View.* New York: Harper & Row.

Ministry of Truth. (2012). An Open Letter to the People Who Hate Obama More than They Love America. *Daily Kos*, January 9, 2012. [Accessed May 28, 2018].

Murrow, E. (1954a). On McCarthy, No Fear. www.youtube.com/watch?v=vEvE mkMNYHY [Accessed May 28, 2017].

Murrow, E. (1954b). A Report on Senator Joseph R. McCarthy: See it Now. www. lib.berkeley.edu/MRC/murrowmccarthy.html [Accessed May 28, 2017].

Murrow, E. (1954c). *Edward R. Murrow's Reply to Senator Joseph McCarthy's "See It Now" Appearance.* (April 13, 1954). www.youtube.com/watch?v=8wMiPkaofjw [Accessed May 28, 2017].

Murrow, E. (1954d). A Report on Senator Joseph R. McCarthy See it Now. *CBS-TV*, March 9, 1954. www.lib.berkeley.edu/MRC/murrowmccarthy.html [Accessed May 28, 2017].

Naar, I. (2013). *Al Jazeera.* www.aljazeera.com/indepth/interactive/2013/12/time line-arab-spring-20131217114018534352.html [Accessed May 28, 2018].

Nee, D., Jahn, A., & Brown, J. (2014). Prefrontal Cortex Organization: Dissociating Effects of Temporal Abstraction, Relational Abstraction, and Integration with fMRI. *Oxford Journals, Cerebral Cortex.* https://www.ncbi.nlm.nih.gov/pmc/arti cles/PMC4184367/ [Accessed October 29, 2017].

Newman, C., & Suchak, S. (2017). Taking Back the Lawn. *UVA Today.* https:// news.virginia.edu/content/uva-sends-message-love-and-unity?utm_source= UFacebook&utm_medium=social&utm_campaign=news [Accessed March 18, 2018].

Nicholson, N. (1998). How Hardwired is Human Behavior? *Harvard Business Review.* 76:134–147.

Oppenheim, M. (2017). Neo-Nazis and White Supremacists Applaud Donald Trump's Response to Deadly Violence in Virginia. *The Independent.* www. independent.co.uk/news/world/americas/neo-nazis-white-supremacists-cele brate-trump-response-virginia-charlottesville-a7890786.html [Accessed March 17, 2018].

Ortega y Gasset, J. (1932). *The Revolt of the Masses.* New York: Norton.

Oshinsky, D. M. (2005) [1983]. *A Conspiracy So Immense: The World of Joe McCarthy.* New York: Free Press.

Panksepp, J. (1998). *Affective Neuroscience: The Foundations of Human and Animal Emotions.* New York: Oxford University Press.

Panksepp, J. (2013). Toward an Understanding of the Constitution of Consciousness through the Laws of Affect. *Neuropsychoanalysis.* 15:62–65.

Partanen, A. (2017). *The Nordic Theory of Everything: In Search of a Better Life.* New York: HarperCollins.

Preston, A. (2013). Interplay of Hippocampus and Prefrontal Cortex in Memory.

Current Biology. www.sciencedirect.com/science/article/pii/S0960982213006362 [Accessed October 29, 2017].

Reed, G. (2001). Shame/Contempt Interchanges: A Frequent Component of the Analyst-Patient Interaction. *Journal of the American Psychoanalytical Association.* 49(1):269–275.

Reeves, T. C. (1982). *The Life and Times of Joe McCarthy: A Biography.* New York: Stein and Day.

Riemen, R. (2018). *To Fight against This Age: On Fascism and Humanism.* New York: Norton.

Sapolsky, R. (2017). *Behave: The Biology of Humans at our Best and our Worst.* New York: Penguin.

Scheler, M. (1912). *The Ressentiment in the Construction of Moralities.* www.mercaba.org/SANLUIS/Filosofia/autores/Contempor%C3%A1nea/Scheller/Ressentiment.pdf [Accessed March 17, 2018].

Sedaris, D. (2018). Personal History: Active Shooter. *The New Yorker,* July 9 and 16, 2018.

Seward, W. (1877). *Autobiography of William H. Seward.* New York: D. Appleton & Co.

Shabad, R. (2017). Trump Says that He's Disbanding Manufacturing Council. *CBS News.* https://www.cbsnews.com/news/trump-announces-that-hes-disbanding-manufacturing-council/ [Accessed March 18, 2018].

Singal, J. (2017). Undercover with the Alt-Right. *The New York Times.* https://www.nytimes.com/2017/09/19/opinion/alt-right-white-supremacy-undercover.html?action=click&pgtype=Homepage&clickSource=story-heading&module=opinion-c-col-right-region&region=opinion-c-col-right-region&WT.nav=opinion-c-col-right-region [Accessed September 20, 2017].

Smith, D. (2017). Trump's Failure to Condemn Virginia Neo-Nazis is Shocking but Not Surprising. *The Guardian.* https://www.theguardian.com/us-news/2017/aug/14/trump-virginia-neo-nazis-analysis [Accessed March 17, 2018].

Snyder, T. (2017). *On Tyranny: Twenty Lessons from the Twentieth Century.* New York: Tim Duggan Books.

Solana, J., & Talbotto, S. (2016). The Decline of the West, and How to Stop It. *The New York Times.* https://www.nytimes.com/2016/10/20/opinion/the-decline-of-the-west-and-how-to-stop-it.html [Accessed March 18, 2018].

Solms, M. (2013). The Conscious Id. *Neuropsychoanalysis.* 15:5–19.

Spencer, H., & Stolberg, S. (2017). White Nationalists March on University of Virginia. *The New York Times.* https://www.nytimes.com/2017/08/11/us/white-nationalists-rally-charlottesville-virginia.html [Accessed October 2, 2017].

Spunt, R., Meyer, M., & Lieberman, M. (2015). The Default Mode of Human Brain Function Primes the Intentional Stance. *Journal of Cognitive Neuroscience.* 27:6, pp. 1116–1124.

Stampp, K. (1991). *The Causes of the Civil War,* 3rd edition. New York: Simon & Schuster, p. 201.

Stewart, D. (1921). *The Participation of Chief Plenty Coups at the Interment Ceremony of the WWI Unknown Soldier Arlington National Cemetery on November 11, 1921.* https://static1.squarespace.com/static/58a2620e8419c2149e7758a3/t/58e30db9 c534a5e980721e3a/1491275195521/Stewart2017.pdf [Accessed December 31, 2017].

Taylor, K. (2010). Obama Hates America and Americans. *Red State.* www.red state.com/diary/Ken_Taylor/2010/07/18/obama-hates-america-and-americans/ [Accessed March 18, 2018].

ter Braak, M. (1937). *National Socialism is a Doctrine of Resentment* (essay), excerpted in R. Riemen (2018), *To Fight against This Age: On Fascism and Humanism.* New York: Norton, pp. 53–54.

The Telegraph. (2018). Timeline: History of the European Union. www.telegraph. co.uk/news/worldnews/europe/6181087/Timeline-history-of-the-European-Union.html [Accessed May 28, 2018].

Theodoridis, A. (2015). The Hyper-Polarization of America. *Scientific American,* Guest Blog. https://blogs.scientificamerican.com/guest-blog/the-hyper-polari zation-of-america/ [Accessed May 28, 2018].

Thrush, G. (2017). New Outcry as Trump Rebukes Charlottesville Racists 2 Days Later. *The New York Times.* https://www.nytimes.com/2017/08/14/us/politics/ trump-charlottesville-protest.html [Accessed March 18, 2018].

Tocqueville, A. de (1863). *Democracy in America,* trans. H. Reeves. Cambridge: Sever and Francis.

Trevarthen, C. (1996). Lateral Asymmetries in Infancy: Implications for the Development of the Hemispheres. *Neuroscience and Biobehavioral Reviews.* 20(4): 571–586.

U.S. Senate. (1953–1954). *Executive Sessions of the Senate Permanent Subcommittee on Investigations of the Committee on Government Operations (McCarthy Hearings 1953– 1954).* https://www.senate.gov/artandhistory/history/resources/pdf/Volume5. pdf [Accessed March 17, 2018].

U.S. Senate. (1954). *Senate Stories: 1941–1963.* www.senate.gov/artandhistory/ history/minute/Have_you_no_sense_of_decency.htm [Accessed May 28, 2018].

Welch, J. (1954). YouTube. Have You No Decency? www.youtube.com/ watch?v=wJHsur3HqcI [Accessed May 28, 2018].

White, J. (2018). Neo-Nazi and White Supremacist groups Have multiplied under Trump, Report Finds. *The Independent.* www.independent.co.uk/news/world/ americas/us-politics/trump-neo-nazi-white-supremacist-hate-groups-southern-poverty-law-centre-a8222351.html [Accessed March 17, 2018].

Whitmer, G. (2001). On the Nature of Dissociation. *The Psychoanalytic Quarterly.* 70:807–837.

Wyatt-Brown, B. (1982). *Southern Honor: Ethics and Behavior in the Old South.* New York: Oxford University Press.

Wyatt-Brown, B. (1991). "Introduction: The Mind of W.J. Cash." In W. J. Cash, *The Mind of the South.* New York: Vintage Books, pp. vii–xxxviii.

Wyatt-Brown, B. (2002). *The Shaping of Southern Culture: Honor, Grace, and War, 1760s – 1880s.* Chapel Hill, NC: University of North Carolina Press.

Yancy, G. (2015). Dear White America. *The New York Times*. https://opinionator.
blogs.nytimes.com/2015/12/24/dear-white-america/ [Accessed April 16, 2018].

Zimbardo, P. (2008). *The Lucifer Effect*. New York: Random House.

Zimbardo, P. (2017). *The Stanford Prison Experiment*. https://www.prisonexp.org/
[Accessed October 18, 2017].

INDEX

ambivalence 37
American Revolution 9, 12
Anderson, C. 20, 21
Anderson, M. 4, 29, 51
antidote to fascism 70
Arab Spring 2
aristocracy, Southern 19
Atlantic Monthly 14
auctions, slave 13
authority, external 74
avoiding complex reality 31
Ayers, E. 22, 23, 36

Baldwin, James xv, 24, 25, 27, 29
beliefs laid down during times of
    heightened emotion 34
Bion, Wilfred 43
blind obedience 53
Boston 8, 55
brainstem 1, 44
Brexit vote 2, 3

capacity for ambivalence 37
CARE xv, 42, 43, 44, 47, 49, 50, 54,
    55, 58, 60
  inborn anticipation 42, 44
CARE unmet 48

Cash, W. 12, 13, 14, 16, 17, 18, 26,
    27, 28, 48
cerebral cortex 1, 32, 44, 47
certainties 1, 2, 23, 30, 46
changing mental worlds 74
Charlottesville 3, 7, 8, 21, 55
Civil War 9, 10, 13, 14, 16, 17, 22, 27,
    62, 63
cleaved mind 32
compromises in number of slave-
    holding states 9
Confederacy 14
confirmation bias 34
contempt 46
convictions 36
coping 45
Covington, C. 24
Crow Indian Tribe 62

Davis, Jefferson 14, 15
default mode network 47
denial 9, 14, 31, 45, 48, 50
denial of prejudice 13
Diaz, Junot 71
Dissociation 31
Donald, D. 28
Douglass, Frederick 25, 70

dregs of European cities dumped on the East Coast 21

economic pressure toward continuing slavery 9
elites 50
emotions impact reality 1
entropic forces 1, 30
European Union 2
evil 13, 14, 24, 25, 74
expectation of care not met 47
experience, painful or positive 45

faith xv, 3, 42, 64
fake news 37, 54
fascism 52, 60, 68, 69, 76
Fellini, Federico 68
French observer of American life 13

Germans 14
Gilmore, James 14, 15
Goodwin, Doris Kearns 12
governmental programs 45
government, too big and intrusive 19
group behavior 37

hatred xiv, xv, 7, 8, 9, 16, 17, 18, 20, 21, 23, 26, 27, 49, 62
hemispheres, development of left and right 46
Hochschild, A. R. 19, 20
honor 9, 10, 17, 19, 22, 62, 63, 65, 66
shame-based 9, 10, 14, 16, 17, 18, 24, 63

idealized past 33
identities 2, 22, 62
insult to the South's way of life 14
Isenberg, N. 21

Japanese 14

Ku Klux Klan 7

Lear, Jonathan 62, 63, 71, 75
Lee, Robert E. 7
Lepore, Jill 70
Lincoln, Abraham 10, 13, 16

Lost Cause 14
loyalties
tribal 1, 2
loyalty to the group 74
Lumpkin, K. 28

McCarthy, Joseph 56, 57, 58
mental integration
dread of xv, 32
Milgram, S. 52, 53
mother-infant 43
mourning xv, 3, 66, 67
Murrow, Edward R. 58
myth
of white supremacy xiv, 7, 9, 11, 12, 13, 14, 16, 17, 19, 26, 27, 32, 48, 62, 65
myth of the chickadee 65

Nazi 7, 9, 14, 24, 26, 27, 52
neo-Nazi 3, 7, 8, 9, 21
Nordic countries 45
Northern attitudes 13
Northern states, slave ownership 12
Northern view 13, 15, 16

Obama, Barack 2, 3, 20, 21
Old South 11, 13, 24
omnipotence 48
otherness xiv, 32
oxytocin 33

Plenty Coups 63, 64, 65, 66, 67, 68
polarization xiv, xv, 3, 7, 22, 27
polarization of North and South 18
polarized positions 15, 71
polarizing pressures 37
Post-Truth Era 50
progressive agenda 2
projection xv, 13, 24, 25, 32, 45, 50, 55, 69, 75
projective identification 25

race 2
racial prejudice 13
reality xv, 1, 2, 5, 13, 23, 24, 30, 31, 32, 36, 37, 43, 45, 46, 49, 51, 54, 63, 65, 66, 69, 75, 76

reality of slavery 12
Reconstruction 15, 17, 18, 19, 21, 24, 32
rescue 27, 31, 41, 49, 55, 72, 75, 76
re-unification 32
revenge 18, 19
Riemen, Rob 68, 76
Ringel, Jack 34

security amidst emotional turbulence 30
security amidst the group 33
self-understanding 1
sense of belonging 33
Seward 12, 13
shame-based honor xiv, 9, 16, 63
shift from entrenched polarization 74
simpler realities 30, 32
simplicity 23, 33
slavery xiv, 9, 10, 12, 13, 14, 15, 17, 62
slavery, costs of 12
slavery, remorse about 18
slaves, value of 9
Snyder, Timothy 52, 54, 59
social pressure to conform 33
Southern
    patriotism 32
    planter class 9
    white working class 9, 10, 12, 13, 14, 15, 16, 17, 18, 19, 20, 24, 25
Southern hatred of the North 18
Southern identity 9
Southern independence 15
Southern planter class 11, 17, 19, 33
Southern succession 14
South, observed to be stagnant 12
Spinoza, Baruch 70
splitting xv, 11, 14, 22, 23, 26, 27, 31, 32, 35, 44, 48, 50, 53

splitting and projection xv, 11, 14, 23, 26, 31, 35, 45, 48, 50
Stanford Prison Experiment 53
stasis 32
state of mind
    pressured 2, 13, 14, 16, 18, 31, 41, 50
    rescuing 69
    sensory-dominated 32

tantrum 49
Tocqueville, Alexis de 13
tormenting doubt 32
tribal 32
tribal functioning 2, 33
tribal modes 75
Trump, Donald xiv, 2, 3, 8, 28, 34
trust xv, 3, 38, 42, 62, 63, 64, 65, 66, 67, 68, 75, 76, 77
tyranny 52

Unite the Right 7
University of Virginia 7, 8
Unknown Soldier 66

Valery, Paul 69
vengefulness 32
violence 22, 27
    internal xiv, 3, 7, 8, 9, 14, 16, 22, 23, 26, 27
violence of language 22

white lash 3
white racism 8
white supremacy xiv, 3, 7, 8, 9, 10, 13, 14, 16, 18, 19, 20, 26, 27, 32, 34, 46, 48, 65
working class 50
Wyatt-Brown, Bertram 10, 14, 16, 28

Zimbardo, Phil 53, 54